I Got Nuthin Strange To Rite

I Got Nuthin Strange To Rite
A Selection of Forgotten Southern Letters, 1861-1865

Copyright © 2017 by Jeff Toalson

ISBN: 978-1-939917-23-2

Cover Design: Jeff Toalson and Jennie Davy

www.palehorsebooks.com
www.jefftoalsoncivilwarbooks.com

Available through PaleHorseBooks.com, Amazon, and Barnes & Noble

I Got Nuthin Strange To Rite

A Selection of Forgotten Southern Letters, 1861-1865

Jeff Toalson, Editor

Pale Horse Books

To T.K.W.

You fired me once and hired me twice.
You were and are a mentor, boss, confidant,
employer, a long-time friend and the person
who created the opportunity for the creation of
Toalson Sales Company.

The Butternut Series

Dedicated to preserving the true history of the ordinary
Confederate soldiers and civilians, by using their voices
as eloquently recorded in their diaries, letters and journals.

Books by Jeff Toalson

Butternut Series:

No Soap, No Pay, Diarrhea, Dysentery & Desertion
A Composite Diary of the Last 16 Months of
the Confederacy from 1864 – 1865

Send Me a Pair of Old Boots & Kiss My Little Girls
The Civil War Letters of Richard & Mary Watkins, 1861-1865

Mama, I Am Yet Still Alive
A Composite Diary of 1863 in the Confederacy

I Got Nuthin Strange To Rite
A Selection of Forgotten Southern Letters, 1861-1865

www.jefftoalsoncivilwarbooks.com

Contents

Introduction

Beryl Markam, the famous aviatrix, wrote, *"[Letters] are keys that open corridors no longer fresh in the mind; but nonetheless familiar in the heart."* There is only one way to bring order out of memory and that is to return to the written word of the participant. If you want to understand the War Between the States you will not find it in the reports and letters of generals and politicians. The path to understanding is with the writings of the ordinary soldiers and civilians. The personal accounts of common soldiers, farmers, clerks, surgeons, sailors, chaplains, farm girls, nurses, merchants, teachers and wives *"open the corridors that are no longer fresh."*[1]

The letters of the common soldiers and civilians were written, in the moment, to their loved ones. They were devoid of posturing and they were not writing for posterity. They were personal and intimate. Many generals and politicians wrote postwar remembrances. Too many of these were decades after the conflict and had a personal agenda. Even their battle reports, which were often written several months after a battle, and their family letters, are not a good basis for understanding the personal impact of the war. Beryl used her flight logbooks, which were recorded in the moment, to bring back the details of items which remain *"familiar in the heart."*

My three previous books used the diaries, letters and journals of over 400 of these common soldiers and civilians. In both *No Soap, No Pay, Diarrhea, Dysentery & Desertion* and *Mama, I Am Yet Still Alive* I used selected portions of letters, diary & journal entries from 220 men and 50 women to tell an intimate, personal history of the conflict. In the process I met many wonderful writers.

Some great letters came to light after the publication of the book where specific writings would have fit. In other instances I was only able to give you a glimpse of the writer. Still others have been found as I have worked on transcription projects of various types.

This is not a book in the sense that it has a directional narrative or even a story. This is a collection of some wonderful letters I found during 15 years of research. Letters that needed to be published and shared with a wider audience. This book preserves their history.

I hope you enjoy these remarkable voices.

1.   *West with the Night,* Beryl Markham, San Francisco, 1983, p. 3.

Editor's Notes

It is my belief that documents lose their historical flavor, and their magical feeling, if the spelling, punctuation or wording is modified. In many cases, because of the scarcity of paper, writers did not use paragraphs. You will be reading the letters as they wrote them. I will not be creating paragraphs, adding or changing punctuation, or correcting spelling.

Many of these writers have unusual habits for using both periods and capital letters. This type of sentence structure is normal: *"Mrs John King died . . . we are going to see Aunt M on saturday."* Periods are typically used at the end of sentences and seem optional in other situations.

Quite often our writers spell a person's name or a place incorrectly. I will put the correct spelling in brackets. *"We are near Vixburg [Vicksburg] camped on the Aszoo [Yazoo] river."* *"Gen Jackson caught up with the enemy at Manassus [Manassas] plains . . ."* Sometimes this is not necessary as in, *"this is one of the worst Lincoln counteys in Kaintucke."*

Certain abbreviations are used on a regular basis: Yr Aff [Your Affectionate], Gen or Genl [General], CH and CoHo [Courthouse], &c [etc.} are the most common. You will see consistent misspellings of recognizable words and phrases and these will not be changed: meessels, enuf, sevrel, prey for us, verry, rashens, git, enuf, and ber footid are some key examples. It is amazing all the ways there are to spell diarrhea and mosquito.

Some of their written thoughts are just magical. Private Nimrod Nash, of the 13th Mississippi Infantry, writes to his wife Mollie, "*. . .I stood the march verry well except my feet they are completely worn out but I can sorter hobble along . . .*" Josephine Robison wrote to her husband serving with the Maury Light Artillery at Fort Donelson, "*John I wish you could see yore little children. Sister can walk all over the house and is as fat as a little pig. She has got five teeth. You sed you wanted to know whether she suckes or not. Yes she does an can say titty as good as I can. . . . John we have not got the meessels yet . . .*"

Those readers who are familiar with my style know that I use [. . .] to indicate that I have left out text before or after other text. There is an example in the last sentence of the paragraph above. I will use [___ ____] to indicate that I have left out two words that could not be transcribed from the text.

I have tried to stay true to the style of the writer and have sometimes wished my computer would quit trying to assume what I am typing. It loves to change befel to befell and thursday to Thursday. It is necessary to go back and correct the computer.

It is my pleasure to offer you these remarkable voices. The thought that they might be lost, or spend many more decades sitting unread in an archival folder, is unthinkable. Every time I read Private Eli Fogleman's letter to Lucy about his smallpox vaccination I start laughing. These letters needed to be shared.

"York Town . . . is a very old and dilapidated town"

Letter of Private Thomas J. Head of Co. B – 6th Georgia Infantry

York Town Va
June 15th 1861
My dearest Sallie

I now seat myself to write you a few lines acknowledging the receipt of your most lovely letter dated June the eighth, and I assure you it was with the greatest pleasure that I received it.

I have been moved as you will see from the heading of this letter to the great place York Town. This place is a very old and dilapidated town there has not been a house erected since Cornwallis delivered the sword to General Washington.

The old fortifications of Cornwallis are very visible in some places I visited his cave the other day, it is situated right on the river banks and it has a hole just large enough for a man to crawl through it is hewn out of solid rock and is about ten feet square inside. We are making great preparations for a fight here. The soldiers are throwing up breast works for a mile out of town.

I have been sick ever since I came to this place but am getting nearly well and who could help from getting well when they get such consoling and loving letters as the one I received from you last night it is almost enough to revive the dead.

We are expecting a fight every day we have been sleeping under arms for two or three nights and we don't know what moment the enemy will attack us. We received orders the other day to march immediately to the other side of town that the enemy was in two miles of this place but it was all a farce. I think it was done to see how the men would stand it. There was about two hundred in the regiment that was excused from duty that day but when the orders came I don't think there was excusing a dozen men who stayed in camp. It seems that they all anxious for a fight. The Virginia and North Carolina regiments had a fight the other day with the abo-

15

litionists and our men killed about two hundred of the enemy and they only got one man killed and five or six wounded. You asked me to write you a long letter I would do it with great pleasure but I have so much to tell you and about so many important things that I hardly know which to write first. And another thing we must not expect a soldier to write much at a time because we are not fixed for writing as we would be if we were seated in our quiet country homes where we have nothing to disturb us. I am now sitting on the ground in my tent beside my trunk writing and my chum laying sick with the fever and some of the boys in the tents near mine are playing the violin and some of the companies are out on drill with drums beating and amidst all of this confusion I am trying to write to the only being on earth that is nearer to me than a Father & mother.

And as you say I hope that the day will not be far off when we will spend a great many pleasant hours together. If I am not with you now my thoughts are ever with thee there is not a day that passes over my head but what I think of thee.

And if I am called out on the battle fields I will remmember thee and the more I think of thee the more I will strive to conquer my enemies. I will know that there is one being that cares for me and one I care for Dearest Sallie you must not think I am a flatterer when I say that you are the most lovely being I ever saw.

You must write to me immediately when you receive this letter for we may be removed from this place in the course of two or three weeks. Write soon, and may god bless you I remain forever your true lover

T. J. Head
PS
Address   T J Head
6th regt of Ga Vol
York Town
Va

(ed: T. J. is a private in Company B of the 6ᵗʰ Georgia Infantry. He enlisted on May 20, 1861, in Dade County, Georgia. The swampy environment, of the lower peninsula, and contact with soldiers with a wide variety of diseases results in Thomas receiving a disability discharge on September 20, 1861, while still stationed in the Yorktown area. He served in Co. H of the 6ᵗʰ Georgia Militia beginning on April 15, 1864, and was discharged from service in Augusta, Georgia, on April 9, 1865.)

(ed: In the middle part of the letter when he writes of the "fight the other day" and "killed about two hundred of the enemy" he was making reference to the Battle of Big Bethel which was fought on June 10, 1861.)

Private Thomas J. Head Letter, SC00117, Special Collections Research Center, Swem Library, College of William and Mary, Williamsburg, Virginia.

"thare isant more than thirty of the company able for service"

Letter of Private John W. Robison of the Maury (Tennessee) Light Artillery

December the 9th, 1861
Kaintucky – Hopkinsville

Dear wife [Josephine]:

I seat myself one time more to inform you that I am not well at this time, hoping those few lines may find you and the children well and in good spirits. I have got the mumps. I taken them yesterday eavening. My left jaw paind me verry bad last night. It is swelt right smart this morning but it don't pain me verry mutch this morning. I expect that I will go to Clarksville tomorrow to go into the hospitel. Thare is about fifty of our company in the hospitel at Clarksville and some eight or ten to go tomorrow. Thare isant more than thirty of the company that is able for service and if we stay here one week longer we will all be sick and enimys will just come and take us.

We are expecting a fight at this place or some whare clost about here. The General gave us orders to be ready to go on a march at one half hours notice. We sent our sick to Clarksville and all of our extra baggage to Clarksville. Some of the familys is mooving out of this place. Thare is a great deal of excitment here about the war. Thare is then two thirds of the citicens in Hopkinsville that is Lincolnites. This is giving up to be one of the worst Lincoln counteys in Kaintucky.

Cooper is well. James Adkerson is in the hospitel. He has got the mesels. John Watson is verry bad of. I dont know what is the matter with him. He has been sick ever since we left home. James

Vestal is sick and has been ever since we left home. He has got the meesels. Bill Willis got his foot scalded so as he can't do anything and I can't take the time to tell all of the names that is sick.

Josephine I would be glad to hear from you and the children. I have not received a letter from you since I have been here. I don't know the reason of it. If you right they don't come to this place. How glad I would bee to hear from you and the children. I have rote to you three or four letters and never received any answer male. I have stood the camp life verry well untill I took the mumps. Though I would be glad to see you and the children ever day if I could the chance but take everthing easy and I want you to do the same thing. Never take more on you than you can help.

Tell Mary to rite to me and tell Hannah I would have rote to her before now if I cud get the paper. I bought two sheets of paper and two envelopes and give a dime for it and could hardly get it at that. I haven't spent verry mutch money. I haven't got but one dollar and sixty-five cents. You must save yore money as best you can. You must rite a letter and send it by William West. You can send me a good long letter. He will stay nearly two weeks and give me all the news that you can.

Josephine I got got to tell you of all the sick. John Skelly has got the meesels. Columbus Hudspeth has got the meesels. They are at Clarksville in the hospitel. They was sent off in the rain. I think they was treated verry bad by sending them off in the rain.

Tell Tommy his Pa wants to see him and Sissy too. Don't let him forgit his Pa. If I live I will want to be at home again.
I remain

Yore loving husband until death,
John W. Robison

(ed: John (22) married Josephine Trotter (17) on August 17, 1857, against her father's wishes. On August 18, 1858, their first son, William Thomas, was born and on October 7, 1860, their first daughter, Mary Angeline, was born. They refer to them in the letters as Tommy and Sissy.)

(ed: The 1860 Maury (pronounced Murray) County census shows John (25), Josephine (20) and Tommy (2). John's occupation iwas listed as a farm laborer. They owned no slaves and had $200 of personal property.)

(ed: John joined the Confederate artillery as a private and was mustered in with his unit on October 16, 1861, near Hopkinsville, Kentucky. They spent several months training in this area before they were ordered to Fort Donelson, Tennessee.)

(ed: Early in the war, as soldiers gathered in various training camps, diseases like measles, mumps and smallpox ran rampant. 'City' soldiers had been exposed to many diseases. That was not the case with the soldiers from the rural areas. These diseases took a terrible toll, on that segment of the military population, in both Southern and Northern armies.)

The John W. Robison Letters, Brewer Library, United Daughters of the Confederacy, Richmond, Virginia.

Mackenzie's Five Thousand Receipts in all the Useful and Domestic Arts

A New American Edition from the Latest London Edition
John I. Kay & Co., Publisher – Pittsburgh
4th edition (undated) – 1st edition published 1829

Page 215:

Measles

"Symptoms – Inflammatory fever, dry cough and hoarseness, sneezing, watering of the eyes, which itch, a running from the nose, great drowsiness. On the fourth day, small red points break out, first on the face, and then gradually over the body. They are in clusters, and on passing the hand over them, are found to be a little raised. On the fifth or sixth day the vivid red changed to a brown, and the eruption goes off.

Distinguish it from small-pox and all other diseases, by the dry cough and hoarseness, by the appearance of the eyes, which are red, swollen, and loaded with tears.

Treatment – The patient must be confined to a low diet, and kept in bed, with as much covering (but no more) as may be agreeable to his feelings. The room should be cool, and if there is much fever and pain in the head, bleeding is necessary. Should there be pain and oppression at the breast, apply a blister. The bowels may be opened by salts. The mild form of measles ought to be treated like any other inflammatory complaint, taking care, however, not to repel the eruption by cold. If this happens, place the patient in a warm bath, give him warm wine &c. internally, and apply mustard poltices and blisters to the feet and ankles.

There is another and more dangerous kind of this disease, which may be known by the fever being a typhus, and by all the symptoms showing a putrid tendency. The moment this is perceived, have recourse to bark, wine, muriatic acid, &c. &c. as directed in putrid fever.

"We went out this eavening to try our cannons"

Letter of Private John W. Robison of the Maury (Tennessee)
Light Artillery

December, 1861

To Mrs. Josephine Robison
Santa Fee, Maury County, Tenn.

Josephine, we went out this eavening to try our cannons. We shot
them eight hundred yards. You aught to see the dirt fly when they
hit the ground. They make a hole in the earth.

Josephine you must save me some butter and milk when you hear
I am acoming. I wisht I had some milk and butter. I am taking on
about it. Would you make me a pair of good thick janes breeches
and two pair of slips to go over my socks and oblige. Josephine
I forgot to tell you that Tom Foster got a clear discharge. I don't
know what is the matter with him.

J. W. R.

*(ed: The Maury Light Artillery got to practice with their can-
non. John did not say whether they hit their targets but they
sure did make "the dirt fly.")*

*(ed: John was already writing home for Josephine to send
him articles of clothing. He wanted a thick pair of "janes*

pants' (denim). The Confederate soldier was seldom clothed in a total gray uniform but rather a collection of items, many from home, in denim, cotton, & wool in varied shades of tans, browns, grays, blacks, dark greens, and light blue. The wives created dyes made from acorns, yarrow, marigolds, walnut peels, birch tree bark, walnut bark, logwood and many other plants and substances.)

The John W. Robison Letters, Brewer Library, United Daughters of the Confederacy, Richmond, Virginia.

Basement Bomb Making Explosion – Richmond, Virginia

Charles L. Powell Letter to family in Winchester, Virginia

Richmond Va Feb 14/62

In answer to your letter which is the next in order entitled to a reply. I have to inform you all of the almost miraculous escape which we have had from a fearful accident, with frightful consequences to Sister Rebeccas friend from poor Mr Hubard. On Thursday afternoon I was sitting in the parlour reading the paper, having left the others at their dessert in the basement below when a terrific explosion was heard, followed in rapid succession by two others. We all rushed to the street. Presently Mr Hubard passed us blackened & bloody. I had heard some weeks ago that he was perfecting an invention of some thing like Greek fire which he hoped to sell to the Government. A few days ago Frank told us it was a fulminating powder & that he had a contract with the Government for filling some shells. _____ insisted upon it, that it involved great danger of setting fire to our house & Frank ought to go to Mr Hubard & protest against his operations in the small house very near to us, when he was doing the work. I supposed that the quantity of fulminating powder he would have on hand at a time would only be a small quantity for scientific experiments & did not share Fred's alarm to any great degree. I thought the danger was mainly, if not exclusively to Mr Hubard, & remarked several evenings ago that he was a D'Alasco who wd [would] blow himself up yet. Frank who is very fond of Mr Hubard, & who had been interested in his success refused to urge him upon the subject, saying he had been assured by Mr Hubard there was not the least danger about it – immediately after Mr Hubard passed us, having taken out Mr Franks we went to the house where he had been at work at which

27

several others had gathered, & found it full of smoke & on fire in several places where the bombs which had exploded had passed through. The day was fortunately very calm, & we soon extinguished the fire. We then proceeded to clear out the papers & litter with which it was filled, lest some lurking fire should renew the Conflagration. Papers & other rubbish were lying charred over the floor. In cleaning it out, Fred came to a box ontop of [a] small cupboard, blackened papers were around it & on the top shelf, outside & inside the doors had been charred by the fire, and on the lower shelf were from 15 to 20 loaded bombs. In the adjoining room, the extremity of which is a yard & a half or two yards from our house & the door of which separating it from the one in which the accident occurred had been blown out by the explosion, were open papers of common powder lying about, several boxes closed & several open half barrels about half full of the coarse explosive powder used for blasting rock, enough if the fire had reached it to have blown our house to atoms & to have prostrated probably every thing else within a hundred yards around us. The gathering of all the material together, the venting of the house & the carrying on such operations without a warning to us, without our knowledge of the extent of our danger (lulling us into a false security) shows a blindness & recklessness amounting almost if not quite to madness on the part of Mr Hubard. Poor fellow, the penalty is very heavy on him. The contents of the shell which he was supposed to have been handling, mutilated him terribly. He had had his thumb & the ends of two fingers of the left hand & his right leg more than half way up the thigh amputated. He has stood the operation well - It seems the pertinacity with which genius near allied to madness clings to its projects, that while in this condition he enquired of his son Willie what had been done with what was in the house & when told that it had been removed, said he wanted everything to remain just as it was when he left it. His family was affectionate & are _____ _____ over & proud of

28

his genius is of course greatly discussed. He has two children a son about 17 a very sensible and good youth about 17 & a bright daughter about 15 years old. Their lamentations were very touching. Mrs Hubard exclaimed that she had lived in constant dread of such an occurrence. "Oh why did he have any thing to do with it!" "Ah! I know it was to put bread into our mouths." His little daughter Ella said "If father had been a drunk and or a lazy man I could see perhaps why this should be so, but that such a man as father should be made to suffer to, seems strange, but perhaps God meant it, to bring him closer to Him."

Saturday Morning. This is a crisis in Mr Hubards case. His system is very much prost[r]ated by the shock & the operation. His head was not wounded, but the missles from the exploded shell passed so near to it, that they passed I think through the rear of his hat which was all crushed & torn away except the part immediately in front – Saturday Night – Alas it seems poor Mr Hubard has paid the penalty of his infatuation with his life – The powers of his system were exhausted beyond recovery. The stimulants which were given him in large quantities through the day could not produce a reaction – Life was gradually & quietly exhausted & became wholly extinct tonight about 9 o'clock. Your Aunts are over there doing all they can to aid & comfort the family – who can not be comforted – They of course can not recognize the fact that so fixed was his infatuation that this calamity has probably prevented a much more extensive one. I thank you for your letter – Good night.

Yr very fond father

C. L. Powell

" . . . they wish to know in time to avoid a draft"

Letter of Julian Burnett of Glynn County, Georgia

Brunswick Ga Feb 16th 1862

To / His Exellency Joseph E Brown
Dr Sir

The County Officers of this County Glynn that is The Sheriff, The Clerk of the Sup & Inf Courts, Ordinary, & Surveyor, have requested to ascertain if they will be subject to a draft to make up the number of troops Georgia is requested to furnish, if the number is not made up by the time specified in your proclamation in case they are subject they intend to resign their Offices and Volunteer. you will please enlighten me on the subject as I am unable to inform them correctly on the subject. and they wish to know in time to avoid a draft.

I am Very Respectly
Your Obt Svt

Julian M. Burnett

(ed: There were certain individuals exempt from the draft in various job classifications. Also, at this early date, men older than 35 were exempt. Mr. Burnett seeks a note from the Governor regarding the draft status of these County officers. These men did not want to be drafted. They would prefer to volunteer for a specific company or command, and not trust where a draft might place them, if they are no longer exempt. Given a choice they would prefer to be in artillery or cavalry versus being in the infantry.)

(ed: This correspondence was mailed to "His Exellency Governor Joseph E Brown" at the Georgia capital in Milledgeville.)

Transcribed from scanned copies of the original which was 'for sale' on Brian Green's bmgcivilwar.com website on June 29, 2016.

"... bring me some butter and half jug of honey"

Late April, 1862: Letter from [Private] [S.] A. Bumgarner
to his brother

Dear Brother I again write to you I hope you are all well I received uncle John's letter and was glad to hear that they were all well tell Grany ever to remember me tell unkle John I am not able to write to him but I want you to hurry and bring me some crout dried fruit and onions and some butter and half jug of honey or a tub of honey you may tell them at home my fare is bad and I want them to help me I will receive assistance from any source so you must help me at home as I mus live on my money at a high rate I have to give 25 cents for one little pie and 25 cents per dozen eggs and one dollar a piece for chickens this takes money as sist us [assist us] while we are sick and save our money you had better come as quick as you can we have letters gone home that we wrote last Sunday tell them all to remember us till we come ____ bring us some dried shell beans to make some bang belly for we like it very well. You need not bring us any corn meal we have corn meal plenty Our men whipped the yankees at Yorktown Va and have taken thirteen hundred prisoners and run them off I cannot give the particulars. I am so nervous I can not write I must stop till rash and [rations]

[S] A Bumgarner

(ed: There are only two periods used in the entire letter. It is like reading a long ramble. However, our writer spells very well even though he is not fond of punctuation.)

(ed: The letter was undated. The only significant battle during the spring of 1862 near Yorktown was the battle of Dam #1 on April 16, 1862. The Union had 163 casualties in this failed attack but camp rumors and newspaper reports could easily spread wild exaggerations. So, lacking better evidence we have dated this letter as late-April, 1862.)

(ed: Early in the letter he writes, "bring me some crout dried fruit and onions . . ." What was crout dried fruit? Well, it actually was three items as in, "crout, dried fruit and onions. . ." On most farms there was an abundance of cabbage and it was pickled and preserved. We would call this kraut but crout is no doubt pickled cabbage or it may also refer to other pickled and preserved vegetables.)

(ed: Mr. Bumgarner is proving to be a bit elusive in the service records. There is not a single Bumgarner, in the records, who enlisted in time to be at Yorktown and whose unit was actually at Yorktown. Further research is required to see if he has been incorrectly listed as a Bumgardner, Bumgartner, or some other derivative. He does want his family to "hurry and bring me" the various food items. This would imply that he was most likely a Virginia or North Carolina soldier.)

Death Notification Letter with Map

Captain Carter M. Braxton – Braxton's Virginia Light Artillery

[Letter to Charles L. Powell, Richmond, Virginia, regarding his son Charles, Jr.]

Near Leesburg Sept 4th 1862

Dear Sir

It becomes my painful duty to inform you that on the 24th of August while engaged with the enemy near Warrenton Springs your son was killed by a shell while bravely serving his gun. He was killed instantly the fragment of the shell striking him on the left side & passing through the heart. I was near him when he fell but before I could reach him his spirit had gone to the place prepared for it. Although he had been a member of my Battery but a short time, by his uniform good conduct & constant attention to his duties he has secured the good opinion & esteem of his officers & had won for himself many friends in the Company. I had him buried near the spot where he fell & it may be some comfort to you to know that all was done for him that kind friends could do under the circumstances – not knowing wheather we were going to hold the field – I thought it best to bury him as soon as possible – I selected a place which could be easily identified & should you or his friends wish to remove his remains before I could point the spot out in person to you – Allow me to say that in your son _____ country lost a brave & noble defender. I believe he died a true christian. Below I send you a diagram of the ground upon which he fell, by which you can secure his remains when you think proper to do so.

[MAP]

We were stationed near the Waverly house (which is yellow) opposite the Warrenton Spgs. Just north of the house in a ravine
north of a brick house will be found the grave of your son in the
plot marked [E^t].   Mr Miller's house is northwest from it – He
could direct you to the spot – I have had to write in great hurry as
I am on the road should you wish more _____ information I will
endeavor _____ __ at another time. _____ Your obd servant I
remain yours very truly

Carter M Braxton
Capt _____ Arty

Chas L Powell., Esq
Richmond

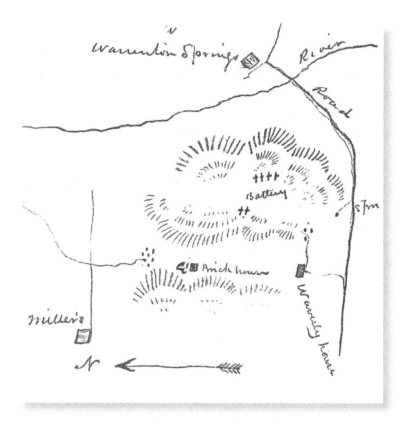

Bottom half of page two: map measures 3" x 3"

Note the mark just left of 'Brick house' denoting the burial site.

Courtesy of Special Collections Research Center, College of William & Mary

(ed: The map is very detailed showing the river, road, Warrenton Springs, the Miller house, Waverly house, Brick house, the ravine and two sets of hills and the position of the battery facing Warrenton Springs. The gravesite is marked with his 'sign' just north of the Brick house.)

(ed: The last half of the final paragraph . . . starting with "I have had to write . . . " is in difficult to read lettering. Captain Braxton was writing in pencil while riding his horse. He was "on the road" and he was trying to finish the letter while on the move.)

(ed: The Powell family lost their first son at the battle of Manassas in 1861 and they have lost their second, and final son, in the campaign & battle of Second Manassas.)

The Powell Family Papers, 65 P875, Box III, Folder 1, Special Collections Research Center, Swem Library, College of William & Mary, Williamsburg, Virginia.

"I lived three days on five biscuit and a little bacon"

Letter of Private Nimrod Newton Nash of the 13th Mississippi Infantry

Leesburg Va Sept 4th 1862

Dearest One [Mollie]

You will no doubt bee surprised at my being at this one hundred and seventy miles from where I was when I wrote you last.

We have been pushing on after the enemy for fifteen days making forced marches every few days. Gen Jackson caught up with the enemy at Manassus plains where the largest battle of the war was fough and give them the worst whipping yet. Hills army to which our Brigade belongs passed over the field day before yesterday. I never saw so many dead yanks on one field.

Our loss was light compared to theirs but still many brave boys have been sent to their long homes. was a complete victory for old Stonewall. Some of the fighting was on the old battle field of July 61.

You would like to know how I stood the march. verry well except for my feet. they are completely worn out but I can sorter hoble [sort of hobble] along yet a little marched twenty miles yesterday but could not keep up with the Regt caugt up about two hours after they camped for the night. feel rested this morning. took breakfast with Mrs. Van deventer verry nice she put some biscuit ham and buter in my Havre sack for my dinner. She is the Lady that we staid with last winter when sick.

We have had little to eat in the march often only one scanty meal a day but not a murmur was to be heard I lived three days on five biscuit and a little bacon marched fifteen miles each day The country is laid waste nearly all the way to Richmond. We will go to Mariland now if I am not awfully deceived no enemy across the river opposite this. Gen Hill has forty regiments here and I can see nothing that he can do but cross and get in rear of Washington. Every one is delighted at the idea of going into the enemies land that is all the talk this morning. The people are crazy at our coming back The Ladies especially. I never saw such excitement among citisens. We have orders to march will give this to some one to send to the south; hope you will receive it soon Jenks [?] Boyd cought up with us at Rapid Ann [the Rapidan river]. I put on the good nice clothes you sent me am verry proud of them have a change of clothes and one blanket with me If we got to Yankey land we will carry nothing with us but one blanket You asked a good many questions that I have not time to answer. We are camped on our old camp ground. Our company numbers only forty men this morning the most of them gave out on the road, will catch up if we remain here long. Give my love to all the friends and relatives and receive the very best love from your

Newton

Dont look for letters from me often

Will write every opportunity

God bless my love

The Nimrod Newton Nash Letters, Brewer Library, United Daughters of the Confederacy, Richmond, Virginia.

Nimrod Newton Nash, Circa 1858

Courtesy of Weldon W. Nash, Jr.

"come and help us fight the Yankees.
Tell all to do thare part"

Letter of Private John W. Robison of the Maury Light Artillery
near Port Hudson

Port Hudson, Louisiana

Nov. the 4ᵗʰ, 1862

Dear Wife [Josephine]:

This is to inform you that I am well and hearty and hope you are
in the verry beste of health. I was in hopes that I could have come
home but they have sent us right the other way so far that it is impossible for me to come home. God send that we may meet again
and that before long. We are on the Missippi River about one
hundred and fifty miles above New Orleans. We are in infantry at
this time but expect we will have to go in the fort and if we go in
the fort we will have to stay at this place, maby all the time. I had
rather stay in the infantry than to go in the fort, for thare would be
some chance for us to get back toward Tennessee. But the most
of the boys wants to go in the fort. They are afeared they won't
get to go in artillery if they dont go in the fort. So if the company
goes in the fort, of course I will have to go to. A fort is a far safter
place, but thare is some danger of being taking prisoner.

I wisht it was sow you could come see me for I want to see you
and children verry bad. I hope the time will soon come when we

will soon meet again. Be of good cheer for I don't think the war will last longer than next Spring or Summer. We can't hold up longer than that I dont think. Tell all the boys to come and help us fight the Yankees. Tell all to do thare part and don't concider them selves slited. If they had have done thare part long ago our country would not have ben in the condition it is in at this time.

Tell Father and family to wright. You must excuse my bad wrighting for I have to wright on my knee and I cant wright mutch, if I have some thing to wright. I must bring my lines to a close by asking you to wright ever chance you have. Back your letter to Port Hudson, Louisiana.

No more, Ile remain your loving husband,

J. W. Robison

Throw these seed in a swampy place. They are palm leef seed.

(ed: The men of the Maury (Sparkman's) Tennessee Light Artillery were being used as infantry. They were transferred from camp in central Mississippi to Port Hudson, Louisiana. Artillery duty was safer than being in the infantry and they would be stationed inside the fortifications manning a battery. The entire unit had been captured at Fort Donelson and based on that experience they balance the odds of capture and prison camp versus the odds of getting killed as an infantryman. When Port Hudson falls, after Vicksburg, J. W.

Robison would be paroled rather than being sent to prison camp. The Maury Light Artillery would not be reformed again.)

(ed: Many citizens would go to great lengths to avoid service. Some secured exempt jobs in supply, manufacturing, railroading, or as plantation overseers. Many would hire substitutes to take their place as they fell within the conscription age range. Some used political connections and were granted exemptions. It became more and more apparent as the war dragged into years three and four that it was a rich man's war and a poor man's fight.)

The John W. Robison Letters, Brewer Library, United Daughters of the Confederacy, Richmond, Virginia.

Mollie Campbell Nash, circa 1858

Courtesy of Weldon W. Nash, Jr.

"for me to come home and see your big fat self"

Letter of Private Nimrod N. Nash – Company I - 13th Mississippi Infantry

Fredericksburg Va Jan 1st 1863

Dear Mollie

In the last you wrote that I must remember you on the first day of the year I write now that you may know that I am thinking of you. We are going on piquet again to night. have our rshions to cook cant write at length. We are duty two days and off four, have had a dull Christmast except one day we got plenty of apple brandy at thirty dollars pr gallon. There is no prospect of a fight at present, but it will not take long to scare up one. There is some talk of going into winter quarters; Gen Longstreet has called for a report of all that have had furlougs, and that have been absent from the command Some think he [Longstreet] is going to give the most deserving furloughs a few at a time. if that is so your man will come in for one; now wont that bee fine for me to come home and see your big fat self. If you are smoking I wont stay with you as long as light as you make of the affair. Well Love you spoke of comeing up. I would bee rejoiced to see you in Va I think you would bee pleased with your visit. There is danger of your taking the small pox; as it is rageing considerably in Richmond and vicinity. dont come until you hear from me again The drum has beat for us to fall in to line must close Tell Bittie ill remember her for macking fun of me That knows she is telling fibs. Am glad you have sold your hogs. you are flush now. will have to draw on you Give my love to all the family. Hoping to hear from you soon I remain as ever your Husband

Newton

47

(ed: What husband in his right mind refers to his wife as "your big fat self?" Well, Nimrod has not lost him mind. In the 1860's it was considered improper, or in poor taste, to say or write the words or phrases: pregnant, with child, and expecting. It is common usage to see writers using the terms 'my big fat self' and 'your big fat self.' Mollie, however, is not pregnant. This is some kind of Newton humor, hinting that if he gets a furlough, then perhaps they can do something to create that situation.)

(ed: Newton will be killed in the late afternoon of July 2, 1863, at Gettysburg, while his command is driving Union forces out of the Wheatfield and back toward Cemetery Ridge.)

The Nimrod Newton Nash Letter, Brewer Library, United Daughters of the Confederacy, Richmond, Virginia.

Smallpox Vaccination and Camp Life

Letter of Private Eli Fogleman,
Company K – 5th North Carolina Cavalry

N.O. 4
I send N O 4 and 5 today
Camp Comfort   Feb the 6th 1863

My Dear Beloved Wife [Lucy]

I take my seat to answer your kind letters which came to hand today and they found me well as they left you and I hope this may find you well I was glad to hear from you and that you was well and harty you stated that you had not been vaccinated & dare not be you wished to know if vaccinating done me any good & if it hurt me much I think it done me rite smart of good it hurt me enough to do some good my arm was sor 4 or 5 days that I could not chop nor hold a bridel It was swelled very bad from my shoulder nearly to my rist the scab is all most ready to take off I think I will take it off & send it to you in this letter you wanted to know if me and John wanted any pillows you kneed not send me any and about John I dont know what to say but I think you kneed not send it I have not saw John since last monday we left the camp near Kinston last monday and the capt left him between here here and Kinston for a _____ as he was not stout the capt told him he thought it would be best for him he is as well as he is for common you said you had only reseived 2 letters from me this year I rote you one, N O 3 Jan the 25th and I answered on that Father sent in _____ to me and yours all so which was N O 3. I think you have got that by this time or I would answer them a gain to day if you got my letter N O 3 I want you to be surtain and answer it, you said

Riley Jones would try and have me detailed to work in the shop with him if I wanted to I would be glad if he would do so for the army is a harable place to be in I understand that all that goes home on a furlow gets in to som shop or other you said Father said tell me that he could not come to see me in 2 or 3 weeks I was looking for him every day while we was at Kinston we left R, C, B and Wm Johnson at Kinston and I left a shirt a pare of drawrs 1 pare of cotton socks and Leonards socks shirt and pants and little thing to send home if Father come or anyone that would take them home safe we drawed 1 suit of clothing and 89 dollars and 60 cts I sent you 80 dollars to mothers by Samuel Hannah you said it snowed at home on the 28th and it was cold wether about home and it is the same way here it commensed snowing on us last Tuesday morning before day we had nothing over us as it rained hailed and snowed till about ten oclock and seased a day or 2 and the commensed raining and rained til a bit a go and it is turning cold now I will keepe Leonards socks if I get to them a gain some of our boys is gon on piket and we will have to go about monday we are 20 miles south of Kinston and 20 from Trenton we will stay here till about March

(ed: Eli has a marvelous writing style that features no punctuation and very few capitalizations. He is writing to his wife, Lucy B. Staley Fogleman, and discussing received and missing letters. Eli numbers his letters so that he and Lucy will know which letters have been received.)

(ed: There was probably more to this letter but this is the front and back of the first page. Any other portion is missing.)

(ed: This is perhaps the best description of a smallpox vaccination I have ever read by any C.S.A. soldier. Because of the unreliable viability of the vaccination material, and also because of the poor diet of the C.S.A. soldier, there were a wide range of reactions. This letter from Eli may not have aided Lucy in her decision about getting the vaccination.)

Letter from Eli Fogleman to Lucy Fogleman, February 3, 1863 - The Eli Fogleman Letters, #5279z, Southern Historical Collection, Louis R. Wilson Library, University of North Carolina at Chapel Hill.

MacKenzies's Five Thousand Receipts in all the Useful and Domestic Arts

A New American Edition from the Latest London Edition
John I. Kay & Co., Publisher – Pittsburgh
4th edition (undated) – 1st edition published 1829

Page 216:

Small-pox

"Symptoms – Inflammatory fever, drowsiness, pain in the pit of the stomach, increased by pressure, pain in the back, vomiting, on the third day the eruption breaks out on the face, neck and breast, in little red points that look like flea-bites, and which gradually appear over the whole body. On the fifth day, little round vesicles, filled with a transparent fluid, appear on the top of each pimple. The eruptive fever now declines. On the ninth day the pustules are perfectly formed, being round and filled with a thick yellow matter, the head and face also swelling considerably. On the eleventh day, the matter in the pustules is of a dark yellow colour, the head grows less, while the feet and hands begin to swell. The pustules break and dry up in scabs and crusts, which at last fall off; leaving pits, which sufficiently mark the cause.

Such are the symptoms of the mild small-pox, but it frequently assumes a more terrible shape, in what is called confluent. In the latter all the symptoms are more violent . . . there is delirium . . . great anxiety, heat, thirst, vomiting &c. The eruption is irregular, coming out on the second day in patches, the vesicles of which are flatted in, neither does the matter they contain turn to a yellow, but to a brown colour. Instead of the fever going off on the appearance of the eruptions, it is increased after the fifth day, and continues throughout the complaint. The faces swells in a frightful manner, so as to close the eyes; sometimes putrid symptoms prevail from the commencement."

(ed: Doctors at the time of our Civil War (1860-1865) used either the term smallpox or variola. They were interchangeable. Varioloid referred to a milder form of smallpox in someone who had already had smallpox or who had had the vaccination.)

"Nothing fit to eat. Corn bread and beef and the beef is dried on foot"

Letter of Private John W. Robison – Maury Light Artillery – Port Hudson, Louisiana

Port Hudson, La., Feb. the 20th, 1863

My dear Companion [Josephine],

This leaves me in good health and I hope those few lines may come safte to hand and find you and the children in good health. I have nothing strange to right. Times is verry hard at this time. Nothing fit to eat. Corn bread and beef and the beef is dried on foot. I never eat sutch beef before. I wisht this state would sink so as the soldiers were out of it. The people of this state has no respect for soldiers attall. They make us pay _____ cts. a pound for pork, lard one dollar per pound, chickens from $1.60 to $2.00. The health of the company is verry good at this time. Cooper is well. Raleigh Dodson rec. a letter from Niley stating that you was well. Give my love to all the connection. Tell Father to right to me, and tell him I will be his true son untill death. Nothing more.

Your true husband untill death. Excuse my short letter.

John W. Robison 1

(ed: The 'dried on foot' comment means the cattle were starving to death and when they were no longer able to stand they were butchered. Private William H. Lucy, of Company G – 3ʳᵈ Tennessee Infantry, recorded the following from Port Hudson, "nothing to feed the steers so we laid a fence rail on the ground drove the steers over it and all that were able to step over the rail let them live all that were so weak they fell we killed them for beef We did this every day untill the whole drove had been eaten by us.") [2]

1.   The John W. Robison Letters, Brewer Library, United Daughters of the Confederacy, Richmond, Virginia

2.   *The Tennessee Civil War Veterans Questionaire,* Easley, S.C., 1985, p. 1398 [Lucy].

"I have cronict dirhea and connot get rid of it"

Letter from Thomas to Mr. Otey, his master,
in Matterson Cty., Alabama

Mount Shell Ten F 27 1863

Dear Master and Mistress,

I will send you a few lines to inform you I am not well but I still get along building stock aids.

Master, I have cronict dirhea [chronic diarrhea] and connot get rid of it unless I could change climate & water.

If you please will you send another Boy in my place I dont think we will get dun with stock aids under two months so I wish you could relief me if you can do so I would rather you wanta come with the one if you could make convenient it is with diferculty in getting off with out wite [white] person.

tell my wife and people all howdy for me I would like to see them all, also you you all Master I give you my best wishes so honore your Servant   Thomas

(ed: Thomas was owned by the Otey family who had land in Meridianville, Alabama, and Yazoo County, Mississippi. Mr. Otey was a merchant and a cotton planter. Obviously, since Thomas could write, he was a valued slave. It would appear

that Thomas was hired out on either a Confederate or Ten-
nessee contract to build some stockades near Mt. Shell, Ten-
nessee. The Confederate government quite often conscript-
ed or impressed workers on 30 day work details but the
length of time involved in the stockade construction would
indicate that Mr. Otey contracted the service of Thomas to
the government for several months.

Because of his chronic diarrhea Thomas was suggesting that
Mr. Otey bring a replacement for the balance of the contract
and bring him back home. He stated that it would be diffi-
cult for him to return safely home without a white person to
accompany him. Paperwork alone would not secure his safe
passage back to Alabama.)

Letter from Thomas to Mr. Otey of February 27, 1863 - The Wyche &
Otey Family Papers #1608, Folder 17, Southern Historical Collection,
Louis R. Wilson Library, University of North Carolina at Chapel Hill.

Mackenzie's Five Thousand Receipts in all the Useful and Domestic Arts

A New American Edition from the Latest London Edition
John I. Kay & Co., Publisher – Pittsburgh
4th edition (undated) – 1st edition published 1829

Page 207:

Diarrhea

"Symptoms – Repeated and large discharges of a thin excrementitious matter by stool, attended with griping and a rumbling noise in the bowels.

Treatment – If the disease arises from cold, a few doses of the chalk mixture, NO. 1, will frequently put an end to it. It is, however, sometimes necessary to begin with an emetic of twenty grains of ipecacuanha, and then open the bowels by some mild purgative, as castor oil or rhubarb. Bathing the feet in warm water, and copious draughts of boneset tea, will be found of great benefit, if it originate from suppressed perspiration. For the same purpose also, from 6 to 10 grains of Dover's powder may be taken at night, being careful not to drink any thing for some time after it. If worms are the cause treat it as directed. When it is occasioned by mere weakness, and in the latter stages of it (proceed from what it may) when every irritating matter is expelled, opium, combined with astringents, is necessary as in the similar period of dysentery. The diet should consist, in the beginning, of rice, milk, sago &c. and subsequently of roasted chicken. Weak brandy, water, or port wine and water, may accompany the chicken for a common drink. Persons subject to complaints of this kind, should defend their bowels from the action of cold, by a flannel shirt, the feet and other parts of the body should also be kept warm.

No. 1 chalk mixture – Prepared chalk, 2 drachms, loaf sugar, 1 drachm, rub them well together in a mortar and add gradually, of mucilage of gum Arabic, 1 ounce, water, 6 ounces lavender compound, 2 drachms, laudanum, 30 drops. The dose is a tablespoonful every hour or oftener. Shake the bottle well before pouring out the liquid, or the chalk will be at the bottom."

(ed: Laudanum is a 10% tincture of opium. The other 90% is usually either wine or whisky.)

(ed: As the diarrhea worsens it become dysentery, or in the advanced stage, bloody dysentery. This is sometimes referred to as flux and bloody flux. The symptoms include, "bearing down pains, the discharge consisting of pure blood or blood and matter, sometimes resembling the shreds or washing of raw flesh, a constant desire to go to stool, vomiting.")

(ed: Mackenzie recommends the use of clisters (enemas) to treat advanced cases. "Clisters of castor oil, with the addition of an ounce of olive oil, and twenty drops of laudanum, may likewise be injected several times in the day." As another option he suggests,"80 or 90 drops of laudanum in a table-spoonful of chicken broth by clister." This will not cure the patient but all of that opium and whisky will make the patient oblivious to his pain and suffering.)

Impressment of Negroes to remove Coal & Wood

Headquarters, District Western Louisiana

Alexandria   April 1ˢᵗ   1863

SPECIAL ORDERS,

No 83

IV   Lieut Manheimer Co F 11ᵗʰ Battln La Vols will proceed in charge of Steamboat *Osceola* to Harrisonburg, and there obtain from Lt. Col Logan a sufficient force of negroes to make an examination of a certain bed of coal located in Catahoula Parish near Mr. Holloman's plantation. The *Osceola* will first discharge such freight as she may have for Fort DeRussy.

Lieut Manheimer is authorized to engage such barges as he can procure for the purpose of bringing out wood on his return trip. He will leave these barges at such points as wood can be obtained at and employ the necessary labor for loading them and will take them in tow as he returns, delivering the wood in accordance with instructions received from the Qt Master's Dept

V   Should the *Osceola* be found unfit for service Lieut Manheimer is further authorized to engage (or impress if necessary) such other boats as will answer the purpose

By command of
Maj Genl Taylor
C. S [?]
AA, Genl

To: Col. Logan

- - - - -

(ed: This is an excellent example of the Confederate Quartermaster Department orders working their way through the chain of command. Wood and coal are required for various purposes. Colonel Logan is ordered to provide negroes for Lieut Manheimer to take with him on the Osceola. The Lieut also has the authority to hire or impress additional labor at other locations to cut wood and load the barges which he is authorized to hire and move to various locations on the river.)

(ed: Armies require huge quantities of food, ammunition, clothing, feed for horses, medical supplies, and a wide list of other items. It is the task of the Quartermaster to provide all of these materials on an ongoing basis. A system of taxes and tithes was in place to accumulate agricultural products for distribution to the armies. However, gaps and shortages occur and must be filled on a local basis. To obtain foodstuffs, plus feed and forage for the horses, details are regularly sent into the surrounding countryside to purchase or impress these items from the local farms.)

- - - - -

Special Order #83 of April 1, 1863 - The General William Logan Papers #1560, Folder 7, Southern Historical Collection, Louis R. Wilson Library, University of North Carolina at Chapel Hill.

"I have had another severe spell of toothache"
A letter from Susan E. Scott, farmwife, near Lake Creek, Texas

May 11, 1863

Dear Husband I received two letters from you yesterday dated 22nd and 29th of April. I had despaired of hearing from you soon feared you had gone to La. I was so distressed about not hearing from you. Garret finally said he had a letter from you and you were not gone said Lizzie got one the same day and I still think it strange that my letters are so long coming. I know that I write every week and will continue to write until my fingers give out whether you answer them or not. I was pleased to hear that you liked where you now are and you were well but I was awfully fear you are in great danger where you are now. I do not see from your description of the place any way for you to get away if attacked. I think it would be a very easy matter for the Yankees to take you all if they wished. I would not stay there if I could help it but I suppose you have to serve your masters. I wish you had not gone there at first remember the Royal Yacht and be very watchful. Our children are tolerably well Garrett has been laid up some time with boils in a particular place he says my health is very bad. I am creeping round so weak that I nearly give out going to the field and back. I have had another severe spell of toothache my face is just beginning to look like a humans again been swelled a week three nights I did not sleep at all. I have not been well for three weeks and look like a skeleton except my face which is fat I weighed yesterday one hundred and fifteen pounds last time I weighed on some steel yards I weighed a hundred and 40. I feel so anxious to have an appetite so I can give milk for the baby. I have taken medicine enough I think but still have neuralgia over my right eye I am now trying to wear it out but it looks like it will wear me out. I think if I could get a _____ _____ from nursing I could get well but I always have a _____ or I am sick myself. Maria [slave] was bit by a rattlesnake again last Monday ran to the house from the back fields never corded her leg [tourniquet] even and the poison scattered all over her by the time she got to the house and I had nothing to put on it until went to the creek for Kiefers remedy. she has been the most swelled sight I ever saw she was bit on her right foot on her little toe and the swelling extended to her shoulder It is leaving now I gave her lobelia and treated as for fever. I was sure she would die but she will get well now I think. She is a great deal better and can sit up and eat the swelling is now confined to her foot and leg I think Kiefers remedy is a failure at least failed in her case. Spirits of turpentine relieved her gave her to drink and rubbed her with it. Squire in the field at work looks as well as he ever did but complains of pain in his breast you know it runs in his family to have pains. I spoke of blistering him again and he got better I think he is well the swelling left his feet and he eats anything he wants without getting sick. The other negroes are well Tom has been stopped work with boils but was not missed I don't think we would lose anything if he had lost all the time he wont do anything unless you watch him all the time wont chop cotton and ruined the stand of corn wherever he hoes. I put him to plowing right by Frank he says he does better there. Our corn is very good in the field near the house it is as high as my head and clean. I have not seen the lower field since it has been worked over but Garrett says it looks as well as this there is a great many burrs in both fields. I try to make the negroes work steady they will get done scraping cotton thursday or friday. There is a great many sick around Mrs John King died last thursday and [Mrs] Betty McGriffins husband died saturday all Browns patients. They are pressing negroes in Grimes & have not been here yet You must come home as soon as you can cough up a furlough the children and I want to see you so bad you have been gone longer than ever before from home. Yours, Susan 1

(ed: You will note that while Susan has excellent spelling she has no use for punctuation and very little use for capital letters. She does not waste any paper by starting a new paragraph but writes, just as she would talk, going from one subject to the next.)

(ed: They rubbed Maria's body with spirits of turpentine. They also gave her turpentine orally. The turpentine was probably combined with a barley water mixture to make it a little less disruptive in the lower digestive organs and intestines. Turpentine was a natural product and was one of the key items in the medicinal kit during the mid-1800s.)

(ed: J. N. Scott served as a private in Co. H of the 20th Texas Infantry and spent most of 1863 in the vicinity of Orange and Galveston, Texas. J. N. will get a couple of medical furloughs in mid-1863 as he struggles with rheumatism. He will continue to have medical problems and will have at least 3 months on furlough in the fall of 1864. The swampy environs and humid climate, in the Galveston area, were difficult for J. N.) 2

(ed: J. N. tried to find a substitute in 1863 so that he could return to his family. He was not successful. In his applica-

tion he noted that he had a wife in poor health, 10 children, 19 Negroes and various elderly family members that were dependent on him and needed his care.) 2

1: The J. N. & Susan E. Scott Letters, Brewer Library, United Daughters of the Confederacy, Richmond, Virginia.

2: Compiled Service Records – Confederate, Micro-Copy 323, Roll 407, Brewer Library, United Daughters of the Confederacy, Richmond, Virginia.

The Imboden-Jones Western Virginia Raid of 1863

4th Sergeant C. Powell Grady - staff clerk with General W. E. 'Grumble' Jones

Hd.Qts. Jones Cavalry Brigade

Near Culpeper CoHo. June 5th 1863

Dear Cousin Nina [Powell],

I expect you begin to despair of ever making a good correspondent out of me, but our irregular life in the service must be my apology for my want of punctuality in letter writing. I found your last good long letter in camp when I returned on the 23 May after being absent for 32 days on our Western Virginia trip. I am sorry that we had not the honor and great pleasure of expelling Milroy from your old home in Winchester or leading him out in bondage but the General seemed satisfied to let Milroy possess the lower Valley if he would only let him stay in the Upper Valley. His troops mostly Valley men, were exceedingly anxious to get hold of Milroy and I believe would have forced him from Winchester at anytime if they had only been allowed to try it. But now our opportunity is gone we left the Valley on Monday last arrived at our present camp on Wednesday and today General Stuart [Gen. J. E. B. Stuart] is having a grand review of his division. I should like to have witnessed it but I had officer duties to perform. I hope we will soon be moving forward now that is the only thing that could reconcile me to leaving the Valley and joining the larger body of the Army. I always like to be with them when they are advancing.

We were all in Western Virginia during the battle of Chancellorsville and could hear no news of the battle except through northern papers. Our loss was great indeed in Genl Jacksons death [Gen. T. J. 'Stonewall' Jackson] but I do not know that it is irreplaceable. His Corps has great confidence in General Ewell and if he is well enough to take command I think his appointment would give great satisfaction. I hope a glorious campaign is now about to open for us. We had a very hard time on our W. Va. Raid and did not accomplish much. I think we failed signally in the object of the expedition viz the destruction of the Trestle [bridge trestle] work on the B&O R. R. near Rowlesburg. We were out of camp 32 days marched about 700 miles or more passed through 23 or 24 counties all this without any wagons so that frequently we were without rations. For seven consecutive nights we were in the saddle nearly all night and the night we crossed the Alleghany (April 25th) the ground was frozen hard. Before reaching Rowlesburg we travelled 36 hours without calling a halt except for a few hours at Greenland, a narrow mountain pass where the enemy about 80 strong sheltered in a log church gave obstinate resistance for several hours killing four & wounding 22 of our men. Col. R. H. Dulany and Major Brown among the wounded. We had to march up to the church (this was about 10 o'clock at night) under heavy fire, break open the doors & windows and throw in burning straw to set the house on fire before the enemy would surrender. We then _____ the even _____ of our way to Rowlesburg after an unsuccessful attack we drew off toward Evansville and struck the rail road again at Independence and pressed on to Morgantown a vile abolition hole which furnishes seven companies to the Federal Army. We then passed on to Fairmont where after 3 or 4 hours fighting without much loss on either side we captured 270 or 300 Yankees and destroyed a magnificent new railroad bridge over the River 900 feet long of which the original cost was $450,000 – we had a job of it that night paroling the prisoners – we had a parole to write for each man and there were very few of us writing. From Fairmont we marched towards Clarksburg and crossing the rail road at Bridgeport within 4 miles of Clarksburg where the enemy had a large force so the General said, we moved on to Phillissas [Philippi] hence to Buckhannon – hence to Western and after two days rest moved on to the Parkersburg railroad & struck it at Cairo Station we then moved onto the oil wells where we destroyed millions of dollars worth of oil and burnt all the engine houses and all the appliances for pumping oil and manufacturing the oil. We burnt a large number of boats containing about 1000 barrels of oil each, beside a great many large barrels of oil. Here we eclipsed the sun and set on fire the Kanawha River and thus ended my work. The dense column of black smoke that rose from the burning oil completely threw Oiltown in the shade and gave the sun the appearance of an eclipse and the oil would run out of the boats upon the water and catch fire. After this our whole aim was to get back to the Valley again and the men were all rejoiced when we again turned our faces toward the rising sun and every body pressed on as eagerly as if they expected to find their home and family in the Valley – they always spoke of it as home – I never saw such a country in my life and never want to see it again. After toiling to the gap of one mountain the only thing we could see was a higher mountain in front of us and mountains all around us. I shall never say any thing against an army that has to operate in that country however unsuccessful it may be or rather however inactive. You have very little idea of the extent of the disloyalty in that country – the southern Confederacy has it bitterest enemies there. After we returned to the Valley there were a good many women & children sent out of Western Va. From Weston and the vicinity – that was the best town that we were in after leaving Moorefield until we got back to Lewisburg. This is a very hilly place and has in it a great many nice people. I made the acquaintance of a very pleasant family there, they were refugees from Wheeling, Judge Fry's family – the old folks were very pleasant & kind and the young ladies pretty & intelligent. I got a letter from Ma dated April 29th enclosing one from Frank dated Fort Delaware April 10th 1863. He had been very sick with Pneumonia but said he was much better. I am anxious to hear from him – It is time he was making an appearance. He does not say a word about Addie the only letter I have seen from him for three years that was not taken up with her – I had seen a beautiful girl in Harrisonburg dressed in goods exactly like that of which sent me a sample before that _____ & admired it very much – I have reference to Miss Lizzie May. She is as sweet as she is pretty. Give much love to all the family for me & believe me ever your devoted cousin

C Powell Grady

Direct correspondence to Genl. W. E. Jones Cavalry Brigade, near Culpeper CH **1**

(ed: General Milroy commanded Union forces in the lower Shenandoah Valley around Winchester and northward toward Harper's Ferry and the Potomac river. The Shenandoah River flows south to north and therefore the northern end of the Valley is called the 'lower' valley and the cities of Harrisonburg, Staunton, Waynesboro etc. are in the 'upper' valley. Quite often writers will refer to the Valley and it will be capitalized. It is a region or an area. This is shorthand for the Shenandoah Valley or the Valley of Virginia.)

(ed: The Jones-Imboden Raid was moderately successful but gained little local support since those portions of western Virginia were very pro-Union. General Jones in his post-action report claimed "that his men had captured 700 Union soldiers, their small arms & an artillery piece. They destroyed 2 trains, 16 bridges, a tunnel, a large quantity of oil field equipment & 150,000 barrels of oil. They also brought off 1000 cattle and 1200 horses which drovers have taken to Lee's army . . . all this had been at a cost of 10 dead, 42 wounded and not more than 15 missing.") **2**

(ed: Fort Delaware is a prison camp on Pea Patch Island in the Delaware river just south of Wilmington. Fort Delaware along with Camp Elmira (New York) and Point Lookout Prison (Maryland) struck fear into the hearts of Confederate prisoners. Elmira and Point Lookout had the two highest death rates of all the Union prison camps. Frank is a little late being exchanged, perhaps caused by his sickness with pneumonia, and that is Grady's concern when he says, "it is time he was making an appearance.")

1. **The Powell Family Papers 65 P875, Box III, Folder 4, Manuscripts Department, Swem Library, College of William & Mary, Williamsburg, Virginia.**

2. *Brigadier General James Imboden – Confederate Command in the Shenandoah,* **Spencer Tucker, Lexington, 2003, p. 134.**

"I am well except my heel where it was blistered."

March 21, 1864: Letter from Lt. Jesse Bates – 9th Texas Infantry

(ed: Lt. Bates has concluded his leave with his wife and family in Hopkins Cty., Texas, and is now headed east to rejoin Ector's Brigade, of French's Division, in camp near Demopolis, Alabama.   They will be transferred to the Army of Tennessee, in northwestern Georgia, in May. This letter details a few of the challenges for a soldier returning from furlough.)

Eight miles below Nachitoches, La.

March 21st 1864.

Dear wife [Susan], I embrace the present opportunity of writing you a few lines to let you know that I am well except my heel where it was blistered. I wrote to you the day after I left you. I wrote from Col. Locks and I suppose that you have got it before this time. I have not got to Scurry's Brigade and I will not go there under the present circumstances. The Yankees are at Alexandria and our army has fell back in to the pine woods South of this. I am with some men that belong to Walker's Division and I am going to send Tom Brecheen's letters to him by them. I have not heard of Agee since he left Marshall. I have spent 78 dollars. I went from Marshall to Shreveport on the carr [railroad car] and stage for 15 dollars and then to Nachitoches for 40 dollars, and I had to pay 2 dollars per meal in some places. I am going to try to cross Red river and go as near east as I can. I expect to encounter great danger, but trusting in God I hope to go through safe. I expect that the Yankees will go to Shreveport. It has rained some and looks very much like raining hard. I feel very sad and lonesome to leave and go through a section of country where I know nothing of the approach of danger. I have to walk with the quarter of my shoe under my foot and if it gets very muddy it will be bad walking. I will write to you every chance. I may not write any more this side of the river, but if there is any chance of send a letter back, I will write again this side of the Mississippi.

I have nothing of importance more to write now only be a faithful christian and don't forget me in your prayers. I hope and trust to God that I will get to my command safe and that peace may soon come so that I can return to your arms. May the blessings of heaven rest upon my dear family. Give my respects to all enquiring friends. May the God of heaven bless us and keep us safe from all harm. So farewell by darling for present.

Jesse P. Bates

to Susan A. Bates and her little children

The Jesse Bates Letters, Brewer Library, United Daughters of the Confederacy, Richmond, Virginia.

"Gen'l G asked permission to bury the dead"

The Cold Harbor letters of Sgt. Benjamin Porter –
11th Alabama Infantry

May 29th, 186[4]
Camps 10 miles north of Richmond, Va.

Dear Sister

I can't think of nothing else but writing. I fear you and Ma are un-easy about me. You need not, make yourselves as well contended as you can. I have suffered a great deal since this war. But have done very well this time. My health has been very good, & all my Co. Leslie Rain has been a little sick for several days, but has been with his Co. nearly all the time.

Sister you think strange of this army being so close to Richmond. I expect Gen. Grant's army is too large for Uncle Bob or we would have fought him any where we found him. We have been on the defensive all the time. Gen. Grant has not attacted us generally since the 12th he turns our right flank every time and will not give us a general engagement.

Both armies have been marching parallel with Richmond for sev-eral days. I think Mr. G. will have to come to the scratch now and when he does, I and all the army officers and men feel confident of success. I never saw men in better spirits in my life. The Yankees have never drove us from a position except one. At day light on the 12th was very sad. We all was sleepy they surprised and killed _____ _____ of Johnson's Division Corps & drove the remainder off. My _____ division was ordered from the extreme left to retake the line and we did so.

We have held every battlefield and I have seen our and the Yankees dead and I know we have killed at leas 5 to 1. Captured there hospital with thousands of them sick and wounded besides those left on the field.

I think God has showed every sign that he is for us, then let us be encouraged. Prey on for prey hath done this great work. God bless you all is my prey. Present my love to all.

I will send you a sheete of Yankee paper.

Yours,

BFP 1

(ed: The battle on the 12th was at Spotsylvania Court House. The Confederate line, at the Muleshoe Salient, was overrun at dawn, in the fog and rain, and most of Bushrod Johnson's Division was killed, wounded or captured. Reinforcements were rushed to seal the breach. The 11th Alabama in Wilcox's Brigade, under the command of General Abner Perrin, helped seal the breach. General Perrin lost his life at Spotsylvania.)

June 3rd 1864
Old Battlefield of Gaines Mill
On Reserve 1 PM

Dear Sister & Ma

Thanks, Thanks to god for his unspeakable blessings.

. . . Early this morning the Yanks made heavy assaults on our left, but was repulsed.

I just learned the Yanks broke our lines about 30 or 40 yards. Our brave Floridians who was in reserve advance to their assistance. I am told but few ever got back with that exception all is well very few of our boys wer killed.

Heavy skirmishing & cannonading continues all along the lines.

My corps is in reserve about 100 yards in rear of the maine line in good breast works all seem more cheerful than I ever saw them. They almost prey for them to come. We get plenty to eat. Half lb. Bacon & bread plenty besides Gen'l Grant let us have a little now and then. I forgot to state that Dan Coleman was severely wounded on the 1st. No one else hurt.

All the boys in fine spirits & willing to fight two to won [one]. Gen'l Grant has done nothing but flank us has never held a single battlefield all their killed & wounded fall into our hands. . . .

Leslie in only medium health. Clay A. as fat as a pig. He always want Yankee crackeers & bacon, suger & coffee. Mr. Heard is well & not a better soldier in Lee's army to be found. Capt. James Hooks, Chs. Griffin all well. . . .

Your affectionately

B. F. Porter 1

(ed: The initial three pronged Union assault at Cold Harbor achieved one break in the Confederate line. A swift counter-attack by General Finegan's two battalions of Florida troops quickly repulsed the men of Barlow's Division, with heavy Union losses, and restored the line.

The massive Union assault of some 60,000 men lasted all of 8-10 minutes and some 7,000 Union wounded and dead covered approximately five acres of ground in front of the Confederate trenches.

Each time the Union army tried to flank the Confederates, by moving to Lee's right and southward,   they left behind not only their dead, and some wounded, but also supplies that were quickly grabbed by the Confederate soldiers.)

June 8th 5 pm, 186[4]

Sister,

As I have not been able to mail my letter since I wrote, so I will try to write more being on reserve where I am permitted to rest partly at ease. My Brigade was releaved last night about 11 pm.

Sis, I will try to tell you more about the flags of truce. Gen'l G. asked permission to bury the dead that lay between our lines. Gen'l Lee after some delay, granted the proposals & the hours between 1 & 9 pm was dedicated to the sacred act. The order to sease firing passed down both lines about the same time. Before this order, ther was a very heavy piquet firing, which had not been entirely silent since 3rd. But strange to say not a gun was fired the hole time. Not five minutes after the flags was seen, our men wer up cherry trees & everywhere else & fearing the Yank in no way.

I was very glad to see those heartless wretches care for their dead one time for they wer getting very offensive. Doubtless, this was the only caus compeling him [General Grant] to care for his dead, with the view also of seeing our position.

I had been on the front line for two day, but did not see half the dead until the armistes was declared. The ground was made black with the slain. Few of our men are wounded or killed. . . . I don't think the last battle is fought yet. It is not known what Gen'l G. will do next. I hardly think G's men will butt us again after seeing our works. Though he may give them whiskey enough to bring them over. I hope the Johnny Rebs will give them a warm reception.

BFP 1

(ed: Military protocol required the commander of the army wishing to retrieve their wounded to send, under a flag of truce, a request to the other commander for a temporary cessation of hostilities for the time required to recover wounded and bury the dead. It took Gen. Grant, as it had at Vicksburg, several days to make his formal request. How many Union wounded died in the June heat without water or treatment for their injuries? It is little wonder that Grant's nickname of 'Unconditional Surrender' had been replaced by 'The Butcher.') 2

- - - - -

Gaines Farm Battlefield of June 27, 1862
Ju[ne] 10th, 1 PM, 186[4]

Miss Jane Porter,

Dear Sister, I feel very well rested being relieved from the front two days. I have given my clothes a cold water rensh and picked off a few confederates [lice]. Sister, I have been round to Lt. Faiths grave and to the place where Mr. Shultz and Simpson lay before they died. It is some distance to there grave. Capt. James was very decently buried near the Gaines House on the same field Daniel James received his wounds. All is well and in good spirits. Genl. G. remaines in our presence yet and it present a disgusting view.

I will send you a Stonwall songstn.
I will close. I want to got to preaching now.
My love to all, prey for me.

Yours as ever,

B. B. Porter 1

(ed: His compatriots, Faith, Shultz & Simpson, were all killed at the battle of Gaines's Mill in June of 1862. Currently, in 1864, they are on the same land and Captain James had just been killed and buried near the Gaines house. This is the reason for the interesting dating of the letter which shows the date for the Gaines's Mill battle "Gaines Farm Battlefield of June 27, 1862" and then the date of this letter of "June 10, 1864" from the same piece of property.)

1. *Prey for Us All – The war letters of Benjamin F. Porter, 11th Alabama,* Ellen Williams, Mobile, 2006, pages 32, 39, 54 & 91-92.

2. *The Civil War a Narrative,* Shelby Foote, New York, 1974, Vol. 3, pp. 290-295.

"... you must not be uneasy about us, we will not starve"

Letter from Mrs. Nannie Key near Helena, Arkansas

September 2nd, 1864.

My Dear Husband: - [Thomas]

I annex to this a few words to tell you something that I know will trouble you, but you must learn of it some time and it may as well be now. Soon after breakfast this morning the Feds (negroes & whites) under Carmichael and Woods (negro colonel) came. Here they were in the yard before we knew it and I had only time to put my purse in my pocket and hide your miniatures when they came in. They plundered everything, searched everywhere for arms, killed all my chickens again, trampled my garden down, pulled up my flowers out of the boxes and broke the boxes, took away every tin and wooden vessel on the place – even to a small tin dipper, carried off my lard, dried fruit, pickles, and vinegar, and broke up all my stone ware (you know we had a good stock), they took all my bedclothes except one blanket and a few sheets, my wool, mosquito bars, all those nice window curtains, my nice table mats, all your letters, papers and deeds, all the children's toys, a good many of my nice clothes, and even Julia's and sisters miniatures, rubbing them out and throwing them away.

The negro soldiers would not even wait for me to unlock the trunks for them to search, but got on them with their feet and jumped on them, kicking them all to atoms. Such cussing, snatching and fighting over the contents you never saw. They held up some of my finest things and shook them at me, laughing and shouting: "She's a Reb! She's a Reb!" They set fire to what wheat I had and the cotton in the cotton houses and burned them up. A great black negro set the cotton on fire. Well, I saved one trunk, thank God.

83

When they threw it out on the ground I jumped up and ran to it just as a host of the black imps were about to kick it open. I put my hands on it and there I stayed with them yelling and dancing about me. One negro drew his sabre on me and another his gun, but I held on until a white man from Illinois took pity on me and carried my trunk back into the house, but even he compelled me to open it and I had to take out all the articles. One black fellow snatched up your cap and went dancing off with it, but the same white man took it away though he did not give it back to me. He asked if you had worn the cap in service. I told him you had. He said he had orders to take all such. They gave all my nice things to one of Aunt's negro girls, Belle, whom they took away with them. They ransacked Aunt's home the same way, taking all she had to eat, some of her clothes, all the mules, and two of the negro boys, Frank and Sal. This is badly written, but the vandals are not far off and I am looking for them to return every minute. God help me! I could do very well, but with the children screaming and so frightened it is all I can do to keep calm. Chesley [5 years old] stood it like a man. He was pale as death, but stood by me, and never shed a tear. But poor little Julia [7 years old], so weak from her late illness, was thrown into a fever. Now to you I will say that you must not be uneasy about us, we will not starve. . . . but I'm not conquered. So like the old oak, the more the wind blows the firmer I stand. Well, all I can say is "Thank God! He is our help and our shield."

Nannie

(ed: Nannie's husband, Captain Thomas J. Key, was in command of Key's Battery of Arkansas Light Artillery in the Army of Tennessee. He received this letter on November 27th when his unit was in Northern Alabama near Tuscumbia. They did not catch up to the army for the battle of Franklin but were with the army for the brief siege of Nashville followed by the defeat and retreat following the battle of Nashville.)

Cate, W. A. (editor), *Two Soldiers – The Diary of Thomas J. Key, C.S.A.*, Chapel Hill, 1938, p. 156-175.

"I was impressed by the idea that you were a gentleman"

Letter from William M. Harrison of Charles City
Country, Virginia

Baltimore 6 Sep 1864

Major General Heintzleman

Sir

You will probably remember that you were at my house near Harrisons Landing two years since – Before leaving my house you kindly offered to serve me if an opportunity should offer – will you pardon me now for reminding you of that offer, & asking you, if it be in your power, to procure the parole or exchange of my son Lieut Thomas R Harrison, prisoner at Johnson's Island who was severely wounded & captured at Gettysburg & has suffered a weary imprisonment for one of his years.

This appeal to you may appear strange but I was impressed with the idea that you were a gentleman who did not speak light & unmeaning words, & I do not suppose my request unreasonable as I have performed the same kindly offer for Union officers – My lot since I saw you has been a hard one; my property destroyed, my family scattered & myself with a son of 15 are here paroled, after an imprisonment which nearly cost the life of each of us. There is no offense alleged against us & Genl. Butler in a long conversation told me that he thought it wrong to take us from our home but that he was compelled to pursue that course to protect his men whom he alleged had been captured by Confederates contrary to the [___] of war – This act of yours will be gratefully remembered if you can do it.

Very Respf
W M Harrison

(ed: An early parole did not happen. Thomas was paroled at Johnson's Island Prison, Ohio, on March 14, 1865, and was shipped to Point Lookout Prison, in Maryland, for exchange. He returned to Virginia and signed his Oath of Allegiance on August 10, 1865, in Charles City County, Virginia.)

(ed: Thomas had been wounded at Gettysburg and went to prison hospitals at Fort McHenry, Fort Delaware and then back to Fort McHenry before arriving at Johnson's Island Prison shortly after August 23, 1863. Prior to his arrival at Johnson's Island his records indicated that he "suffers from his wound." The reports did not provide specifics.)

(ed: William M. Harrison and his son Edward, civilian non-combatants, were held in prison at Fort McHenry, in Baltimore, without charges.)

(ed: The W. M. Harrison farm, near Harrison's Landing, in Charles City County, Virginia, was completely destroyed. Mrs. Caroline Harrison and 7 children, ranging in age from 3 to 15, were relegated to the farm manager's cabin. The 30 Harrison Negroes became refugees and were cast loose with no source of food, shelter or support. Union forces stripped the house and barns to their foundations. The troops used

what materials they could and burned the rest. No remu-
neration was ever provided. W. M. Harrison never regained
his health from his time in prison. Combined with the stress
of being a refugee and the total destruction of his property
it led to his early death. He died September 12, 1865, at the
age of 48. Thomas would work on rebuilding the farm and
that would be such an arduous project that he did not marry
until 1885 when he was 43.)

(Compiled Service Records – Confederate, United Daughters of the
Confederacy, Richmond, Va., Micro Copy 324, Roll 217 & 604; Micro
Copy 331, Roll 120; U. S. Census Reports, Ancestry.com, (1850) M432-
951, (1860) Slave Census, (1860) M653-1352, (1870) M593-1639.

Caroline Lambert Harrison on the porch of the farm manager's cabin with her son John S. Harrison, circa 1880-1885

Courtesy of Madeleine Eckert and William M. Harrison, Jr.

The Wounding of Capt. Richard Watkins at Tom's Brook

A letter from Lavalette Dupuy to her friend Nina Powell

Linden Nov 2nd 1864

My Dearest Nina

Methinks I hear you softly exclaim to yourself "What is the matter with Lettie that she does not write? Can there be any diminuation of her affections for me?" Do not I beg of you think that I for a moment forgot that my dearest friend is separated from me many miles and that letter writing is the only means of communication we have meager as it is, My old habits of procrastination have seized hold upon me of late and amid a multitude of cases that have devolved upon me of late I find it hard to shake off the evil spirit. You will be sure to ask what _____ I, a young lady of _____ of _____ age, can have that interfere with my _____ correspondence with friends and I feel bound to answer.

First, Brother [Captain Richard Watkins – Co. K – 3rd Virginia Cavalry]; as perhaps you have heard, was shot through the hand several weeks since and is now at home and requires Sister Mary's constant attention at his bedside so the care of the children falls to me, & secondly Mamma and Brother has both been deprived of their overseers, and a good deal of the house-keeping falls upon Nannie and me and besides this I have been riding over nearly every day to Brother's to superintend affairs there, so you see I am not entirely without excuse for any tardiness and hope I have satisfactorily dispelled any distrust you may have felt toward me,

91

tho I believe you are too well assured of my love do not doubt for a moment its undiminished continuance.

Brother still suffers most excruciatingly at times and is never entirely free from pain. He says he never before conceived of suffering. He was shot in the lower part of the hand near the wrist, the ball passing entirely through the hand and breaking the bone that connects with the little finger and probably another one. He suffers now as much with his shoulder as his hand, caused by neuralgia I expect. He has been closely confined to bed, his nervous system being much deranged but his general health is better now and he sits up in a rocking chair most of the day but walks about very little. Willie Purnall [Dupuy] was slightly wounded in the shoulder in the same fight [Tom's Brook] and got a pleasant furlough of 40 days, I wish you could be here now that you might see him. I think he is more serious than formerly, I expect he feels very keenly the loss of his dear Mother, and this is his first visit home since her death. Cousin Anna and Aunt Jane are still living there and Miss Boyd has resumed her school. I miss Cousin A. very much and do not see her very often. Aunt Jane is losing her eye sight very rapidly and she is very low-spirited about it. She can neither see to read or knit now, which is a great deprivation as she used to read a good deal. Uncle Joe is in a peck of trouble now, has a dreadful and incurable distemper among the horses and has already lost two of his finest animals and another is now sick. Nannie very agreeably disappointed us in not having the fever, tho tis not too late for us to take it as we have now eight months since it first made its appearance in our midst. Under the Good Providence of God we have only lost two with it and they were among the first cases. Capt. Robert Smith has a very sick family and he has lately been sent to the Army. A pretty effectual drain has been made upon the male population in this region and the few who remain are quaking I believe. Billie McGehee our constant hobby, has gone at last and joined Capt. Flournoy's Co. [in the] 56th Va

Reg. Tis rumored that he and Alice Cobbs are to be married tho I scarcely give credence to the report yet. Charlie Flournoy spent Saturday night with us, He has been sick with chills and fever and has not been with his Co. for some weeks. He enquired for you as he always does. I wanted to tease him about Lizzie Womack but did not dare to. He told me that he believed Bettie Henderson has captivated the wounded soldiers at her Mother's, I should like to hear something more of the Maryland soldier that you met on the cars on your way to Richmond. I received a letter from Cousin Johnnie last week in which he sent a note to you which I shall enclose in this. He is now in Americus, Ga, his wounds healing and his health improving. He expects to come on the Va. In a few weeks and hopes to see you while here. Be sure to come up Xmas, I hope you will meet with an escort. . . . Give my love to your Father and Mother and Lester Beck and Hattie when you write and believe me always

Your loving

Lettie

Excuse Confederate paper, I am without other.

(ed: Richard Watkins, whom Lettie refers to as 'Brother,' was her brother-in-law. He married Lettie's sister Mary. All relations were referred to as brother, sister and cousin. It can be quite confusing at times.)

(ed: The C.S.A. medical records normally would note 'GSW left wrist'. The records noted broken carpel bones and damaged sinews but gave no reference to the type of wound. Until this letter was found we assumed Richard received a saber blow to the wrist. Anyone who has read the Watkins collection of letters in 'Send Me a Pair of Old Boots & Kiss My Little Girls' will now have more detailed information of

Richard's wound that ended his military service.)

(ed: Lettie referred to typhoid fever which was a constant scourge. In 1863 Prince Edward County had been the victim of a whooping cough epidemic that caused many deaths on the farms.)

The Powell Family Papers 65-P875, Box IV, Folder 4, Special Collections Research Center, Swem Library, College of William & Mary, Williamsburg, Virginia.

"I got a pice of mule neck in my mouth"

Private Joseph P. Hoover Company D – 45th Tennessee Infantry

. . . arrived Rock Island prison 11th Dec. 1863 sick and worn out . . . sent to hospital next morning . . . treated very well . . . I were appointed nurse for a while . . . taken the small pocks . . . sent out to the pest hospital stayed about a month with some where about one million or more cooties chasing each other up and down my spine and now an then stop to dig into the small pock sores . . . it was awful. got back to prison pen and to my barrack No. 29 near the middle of the prison . . . that was Apr. or May . . . I could get plenty to eat at that time coffee loaf bread hominy molasses potatoes rice vinegar pickle beef or pork or mule sometimes bacon and sugar . . . order came to cut some of the rations . . . was done . . . gave a call for volenteers for the navy about 400 went out at once they cut the rations off then to 8 oz. of bread about 2 oz. of green beef that you could throw 25 feet against a wall and it would stick. no coffee no potatoes no hominy . . . nothing . . . only the bread and beef or mules . . . I got a pice of mule neck in my mouth and the hair in the meat scratched the roof of my mouth like it was briars I have known men to give their meat rations for a bone when they would beat it up put it in a cup with water and boil and boil when cold skim off the greast and enjoy it. I have seen prisoners get an old bone and suck it jest like I have seen children suck a candy stick . . . when they had starved us this way for a while they gave a call for volunteers to go the frontiers . . . giving them 100 dollars bounty 15 dollars per month . . . feed and clothe them royally and for them never to have to fight the south . . . the result over 1700 went out first call . . . 2 or 3 weeks after this they gave another chance to join them . . . 75 went . . . more calls . . . then no more

95

calls . . . no more food were allowed . . . guess they thought what remained were pretty true Rebbels. if the light in a stove flared up anytime of night Bang went a gun . . . 2 or three killed that way . . . if a soldier had to be punished they had the means right at hand for they had 2 post about 6 feet from each other sunk in ground a 2 inch plank nailed to them with the edge up . . . made to shape a horses head and tail called Mulligins Filly . . . if prisoner had to ride and seemed sorta cowed he got off pretty easy but if he showed the least like it was fun they would tie a 6 lb. rock to each foot . . . bring tears to his eyes and curses to his lips . . . another mode were to tie them up by the thumbs a spike driven into a post a stout string secured prisioner made to stand on a plank . . . hands high as he could reach . . . string fastened to his thumbs . . . blood run from the poor elbows to the ground . . . I get made [mad] everytime I think of these things . . . there were 12000 prisoners arrived at Rock Island, 400 joined the navie, 1763 joined the frontier, 4427 died, 45 killed or missing, 75 at another time joined the frontiers (6810 total left 5190. we had 5190 starved prisoners to come home and struggle for a living but we had the nerve . . . while in prison we eat dogs rats mice and anything but a blue coat I was released from prison 24th March 1865 . . . a prisoner for 16 months lacking one day . . . arrived home 7th April 1865 . . . found my poor old Father in prision at Murfreesboro held as hostage for some carpet baggers the confederates had taken off he was released 17th April 1865 . . .

(ed: Private Hoover was captured at Chattanooga in late November, 1863. He was held in a temporary POW camp at Chattanooga, transferred to Louisville and then shipped to Rock Island, Illinois, where he arrived in early December. He would spend almost 16 months in prison at Rock Island.

Joseph was from the Bellbuckle, Tennessee, area and enlisted in October of 1862. His first battle was the battle of Murfreesboro. Joseph wrote that he served in "Breakerridge Div. afterward in Stewards." He would spend more time as a prisoner of war than as an active soldier in the Confederate army.

He farmed postwar near Murfreesboro. Joseph proudly noted, at age 80, that his eyes were sharp and "still no spectacles.")

(ed: We should not take his numbers as being totally accurate. Some are probably quite close. It is a fact that 1,976 Confederates are buried in the Rock Island National Cemetery. These graves were the beginning of what would become the National Cemetery. Virtually every grave is marked with the soldier's name, unit and date of his death. They are laid out in numerical order. 1,850 of these men died of disease and malnutrition as noted on the Rock Island National Cemetery website. They fail to mention that the other 126 were murdered by the guards. For more details you can read accounts by various Confederate prisoners in "No Soap, No Pay, Diarrhea, Dysentery & Desertion." *)*

Tennessee Civil War Veterans Questionaire, **Easley, 1985, vol. 3, p. 1143-1146 [Hoover].**

"Your money I invested, with what I had in Sugar"

The Alabama Letters of Riverboatman Carter Coupland

- - - -

Carter Coupland was the son of Carter Harrison Coupland and Juliana Ruffin Coupland. He was born in 1831. His father died in 1833. Juliana remarried to a Mr. Dorsey and moved to Alabama. Juliana returned to Virginia, as a widow, and purchased property in James City County (near Williamsburg) in 1858. John Coupland, her oldest son, and his family, lived in Williamsburg. Carter Coupland stayed in Alabama where he plied the rivers of Alabama as a crewmember on riverboats. In 1860 Carter would have been 29 years of age. In the 1850 census Carter was shown as a clerk. I have not found him in the 1860 census. From the letters you get the impression that Carter was not part of either the engineering or the deck crew. Most likely he ran the business end of the riverboat and was in charge of cargo, passengers, monies, and the procurement of supplies for the boat. With his background as a clerk this seems logical.

Riverboats provided a key method of transportation between the major cities in Alabama. During the war they were a key mover of troops and supplies. Civilians were allowed to book passage if space was available.

The following letters provide a glimpse of life on riverboats. This is the only group of letters I have encountered dealing with this important method of transportation.

Steamer *Dalman*
Jany 1ˢᵗ 1860

My dear Mother –

A happy New Year to you & all at home! – We left Montgomery this evening & as I am nearly through work for the night & the Passengers have retired, leaving me a little quiet time, my thoughts turn to you & the dear ones at home – I managed by the aid of a cab to take my Christmas dinner with Jn Marshall & I can assure you I did enjoy it amazingly! - Mollie is looking thin, but is very cheerful & the Baby she says is doing finely – I did not take the trouble to look at the brat; told her I would when it was two years old; - I am at work again as you saw by this, but old Rheumatism has got me still; I can manage to creep about, but suffer a good deal – I could not afford to pay a clerk 38c a week to do my work – I must try & brave it out – I hope it may remain in my legs, for if it gets in my arms the thing will be out with me & no mistake – I will mail this at Selma – Give my affectionate love to all – If you do not hear fm me regularly you may know it is on account of business – Good bye my dear Mother

Your Aff Son
Carter

- - - - -

Steamer *Beulah*
Nov 23d – 61

My dear Mother

I arrived in Montgomery last evening the 22-, but did not have time to write you a line, so will drop you one now & mail it at

Selma. I had rather an uncomfortable trip out, being shut up in the cars with sick soldiers, but being accustomed to the ills of life I stood it very well & now that I have taken a good wash, put on clean linen etc, I feel all right again – My cold is much better & I did not suffer with it as much as I expected. I am very well now & my friends were very glad to see me – will write you again soon – have not time to say more at present –

Your Aff Son

My aff love to all - Carter

- - - - -

Mobile Mch 21, 1863

My dear Mother

I did not go up on the Boat this Trip – as I did not feel very well, having had a chill or two & some slight high fever – But I feel all right today having had Dr. Ketchum [_ _ _ _ _] of me - & the few days rest I will get will benefit me amazingly – Do not be at all uneasy for I am doing first rate & should not have mentioned that I had been unwell except that several Greensboro people came down with me & went up on the Boat & I am afraid they might report me sick –
I got a long & aff letter from Brother this morning written Feby 16ᵗʰ – They have all been Sick since you left but were well when he wrote. – Oh! How I wish they could get out of Yankee Land! There is nothing of interest here – Everybody expecting to Starve – Provisions are enormously High – Flour $80.00 a Barrel. Beef from 50 to 54c for lb   Turkeys 6 to 7 $ apiece - & every thing

else in proportion – God bless you my darling Mother. I must say farewell – I long to see you, but don't hasten your visit on my account – I have written to Hattie Several times lately – but have not heard a word from her – Got a very kind & friendly letter from Jno Hinley also several from Miles – they both asked to be particularly remembered to you – John had received your letters and says it shall be attended to if possible – I will go up & see Mollie this Evening – She has not moved out to her new home yet, expects to do so in a few days – Write to me soon

Your Aff Son

Carter
Give my aff love to Tiff & the children

- - - - -

(ed: His brother and family lived in Williamsburg, Virginia, which had been under Federal control since May, 1862. They wanted to move to Richmond but John needed to find some type of employment.)

- - - - -

Greensboro Oct 11, 1863

My dear Brother –

Your last & much prized letter came to hand some time ago & I should have answered it sooner but for my being taken sick. I was quite sick for two weeks in Mobile with Typhoid Fever & it left me so weak & debilitated that I determined Mother and Cousin Tiff a short visit in hopes the change might do me good – I am improving & will soon return to work again. They don't seem to think that the Boat can run unless I am about – I was truly sorry to learn of your bad health & you have my heartfelt sympathy in all your afflictions – Oh that it was in my power to relieve the sufferings & hardships of your dear little children – brother get them away from Wmsbg if it be possible – I do not know that any suggestions of mine would aid you, but will leave that to the better judgement of yourself & Mother – I think your plan of renting a cottage on the R Rd is a good one; I will do all in my power to help you along, and you must not hesitate to call on me – for you are as welcome as I am – I have been here two days & will remain 4 or 5 more – I am in hopes by that time to be strong enough to go to work –

Give my love to Jno Hinley   Oh! How I should like to see the old Fellow! Also love to Miles – Write soon – Yr Aff Bro – Carter

- - - - -

Steamer *Senator*
Nov 8. 1863

My dear Mother

This is a beautiful Sunday morning & while I am nearing Selma with 450 troops, I can imagine your [_ _ _ _] household preparing for church – I am well & doing well – have no right to complain, but oh! I am sick & tired of the life I am leading! I think there is a better day in store for me yet – Last week I received a letter from Harriett – she was in James City. had not been able to see her Mother, but hoped to do so in a few days. She did not know what her plans would be for the winter. I wish it was in my powers to be her protection. – I feel for her dependent situation – She mentions that "Uncle John" is soon to be married, but says nothing more about it – said she intended writing to you in a few days – My letter was a month reaching me – I keep as warm as a toast under cover of your nice Yarn Shirts – many, many thanks for them - ! Give my aff love to Cousin Tiff & the children – Aunt Sally Uncle Tom &tc – not time to say more –

Your Aff Son
Carter

- - - - -

Selma Nov 24 1863-
Str *"Reindeer"*

My dear Mother –

I have received your last letter – of Nov 12th. Have not time to answer now, only drop these few lines in a great hurry to let you know I am very well – Capt Baldwin has sold the *"Senator"* & we are running the *Reindeer*. She is one of the nicest boats on the River – just as fine as they ever make them! I wish you could come & take a trip to Mobile with me. We leave Mobile on our regular day Friday & Selma every Tuesday Morning. John Marshall is at Mrs Jayses & doing very well, he was severly wounded, but is recovering fast – was up last trip & moving about in the house – I will write in a few days –

Yr Aff Son

Carter Coupland

We heard they are fighting
Sure the mischief at Chatanooga
No particulars as yet – I hope
Bragg will move them - !

- - - - -

Steamer *Reindeer*
Selma Mch 5 1864

My dear Mother,

I have neglected to write to you for some time, but it has not been because of forgetfulness, for I think of you night & day & wish the time may soon come when we can be together as long as life lasts – Mother, I have had a hard time lately. – As much work as two men ought to do, but, I manage to scuffle through & I dont complain a bit, for these are war times! – We have been carrying troops for the last three weeks & you can imagine what I have gone through with – no rest night or day - ! John & Mollie came up with me trip before last on their way to Virginia – I had that trip about 400 passengers. Principally ladies and children – of course I could not see much of them – I think Mobile is at present one of the safest places in the Confederacy.

Your money I invested, together with what I had in Sugar. I think I will dispose of it when I get to Mobile provided, I can double my money – Sugar I consider a Luxury & therefore I do not think it wrong to speculate in it – I could write you a long letter but have not the time – Excuse this scratch & all mistakes – for I have been up all night –

I got a letter from Harriette. Perhaps the last I shall ever receive! in which she requests me to ask you to write to her.

Yr Aff Son
Carter

Her Post office is,
B[_ _]ington P O
King & Queen Co.
Care   R. G. Henly
Oh! You do not know
my dear Mother how
I long to see you

- - - - -

Montgomery July 12/64

My dear Mother -

Your letter dated Columbus June 23.d reached me in Mobile – I was delighted to hear once more from you, for in these trying times a letter from your Mother cheers the heart. even if things look so gloomy! I have not heard a word from Va. – Oh! how it does sadden the heart, to be in such suspense – In God alone must be our trust - - Everything at present looks gloomy: - but we must hope for the best –

I am very glad Your visit was a pleasant one – You did not mention when you were going to return – I shall write to Greensboro, hoping this may reach you – The *Reindeer* has laid up & I made

two other trips on the *Senator No. 2* – I then stopped off to settle up business - & am now in Montgomery for that purpose – I shall have to return to Mobile & it may take me several weeks to get through, when I do. I intend trying to come & see you – for Oh! how I do long to meet you again – I will deliver your note to Mr. Wheelen, as soon as I get to Mobile – Give my Aff Love to Tiff & the children
Youre Aff. Son
Carter

The Board gave me
a full discharge

(ed: The army may have been trying to conscript Carter. Either his long time career on riverboats or his medical problems earned him "a full discharge." He would continue his work on riverboats for the balance of the war.)

- - - - -

Selma Aug 9th / 64

My dear Mother –

I left Mobile Saturday evening. The greatest excitement was prevailing in the city. We have a hard road to Travel! but I think it will be some weeks before the Yanks will make an attack by land! – I had business here, & thought it best to come up & settle it – as they are putting everybody in the trenches –

I was not able to do duty; but it may look as if I was not willing to do what I could toward defending the old town. So instead of a pleasant visit & joyous welcome from my dear Mother I must return to strife & excitement. Dont You think I am right. it may be that My Services will not be needed – if so, You shall hear from me soon – No noncombattans are allowed to enter the city – but all are ordered off from there.

I got a pass to come up to meet my Boat. I will leave here tomorrow morning - & if there is any chance, & I can honorably leave, I will come & see you soon –

My Aff love to All –

Yr Aff Son

Carter

- - - - -

Str "*Dixie*" Aug 27/64

My dear Mother

Your last letter enclosing one from Brother, has been received. both of which were read with much interest & prized as you are well aware that all your letters are – You did not say anything about your health. I have been fearful you were not well & would not let me know of it - -

Your letter enclosing Brothers which was sent by Jno Goldthrush came safely to hand, & I answered it; but suppose you never received it – I collected from Mr. Wheelen $160.00 for you - - I had to remain in Mobile some time and I am flat broke. it take a small fortune to live a few days these times – I am without shoes & pretty nearly without clothes, but will try & scuffle through.

Our Hlds [holdings] of Sugar, will probably pay You the amount of the money invested, that is in new issue, which will be a profit of 33 1/3 on the dollar – There has not been any demand for Sugar, for a long time, and the loss in weight, together with Taxes, I am afraid will not more than bring you out even – I believe if I was to invest in a Gold Mine, Gold would be worth nothing in a short time.

I could not get Your Sugar out of Mobile, so had to run the risk of the Yankees taking our little stock - – left it with a good house & told them to sell it as soon as possible – I am disappointed in the quality, twas not as good as the sample I purchased by –

Mother nothing would give me more pleasure than to contribute in the slightest degree to my dear Brothers comfort & necesities; but at this time I have not money enough; I would have to pay $4.00 for a lb of Bacon, & as I said before, I am without funds – The Government is paying nothing, they the Q.Masters have had no money for 6 or 7 months, and consequently the boats have received nothing for their services –

Brothers letters will be well taken care of – My Aff Love to all

Yr Son
Carter

(ed: His brother John and family have moved to Richmond near the railroad. At this point virtually everyone in the Confederacy was in dire straits. Carter had no monies for assisting other family members.)

- - - - -

Str *Dixie* Sept 9. 1864

My dear Mother

Your letter of the 1st inst has just been received – enclosing the one from Aunt Jane which was very interesting. I am very glad you sent it; I have not heard anything from them for so long – Your letters now are my only comfort they always cheer my gloomy heart - & I look for them as my only comforter –

I do not think I wrote you that I had received a letter from Brother: Also one from Miles; both have been written more than a month ago – Brother says that Harriet had just arrived from King & Queen [County, Virginia] & was staying with them – Miss. Mattie was also there & her health very bad. His wife & children were well but he is suffering with his old complaint; the Liver, Says he only weighs 117 lbs; poor fellow I feel very sorry for him – Many thanks my dear Mother, for your kind offer to mend my clothes – I will send to Mobile & get my old stock sent up. My flanel shirts are all good so are my socks – my draws are so small & short I cant get into them – I have ½ Doz good shirts the balance are worse for wear, but two of them might make one good one – I will try & come to see you as soon as possible. Capt. Locklier is now at home, when he returns, I will try & beg off for a few days – Will let you know when I can come - - Good brown Sugar is worth in Selma 4.00 per lbs & all sold at that – I expect you can do better with it in Greensboro – Henry Casey is still on the "*Dixie*" with Capt. Finnegan. I will collect his hire the first time I meet the Boat in Selma or Montgomery – provided there is any money to be had for they are like all the balance of us flat broke – the Govt has not paid any of them for 8 months – Give my aff love to Tiff & the children & remember me to Uncle Tom & Aunt Sally – Yr Aff Son –
Carter

(ed: Carter's mother, Mrs. Juliana Dorsey, was a refugee from Williamsburg. While she stayed with several different relatives, the majority of her time was spent in Greensboro, NC, with Cousin Tiff and family.)

- - - - -

Str. *Dixie*
Sept 28, 1864

My dear Mother -

Your letter enclosing one from Harriet has been received. I was very glad to hear from her, for I have received no letters from her & was very uneasy about her – I have written repeatedly to her but presume my letters were lost! Thank God she is well! - - I hope to hear from her soon - - I had hope to have been to see you before this; but business requires me here, the war times we are not our own masters – Capt. Lockliers Family is sick & he wants to go home, I don't know when he can get off – but probably this week, as soon as he returns I am coming to see you, it may be 2 or 3 weeks yet – Oh! How I do long to see you again – I will bring my clothes with me that need repairing & will try and spend a week with you – I have not time to write more.

Yr Aff Son

Carter

- - - - -

Steamer *Dixie*
Demopolis Oct 13, 1864

We may have to be up here
for some time – I will try
to get off about the middle
of next week – But don't expect
me until you see me –

My dear Mother –

We were ordered from Selma to this place & have made our Trip up the Bigbee River – I have been all alone Capt Locklier having been at home with his Family; he arrived here Yesterday & will take command, much to my relief, as the responsibility is rather too much, being unacquainted with these Rivers – We will leave this evening for Gainesville or thereabouts for another load of corn – when we return we may be ordered back to Selma, if not I am coming to see you anyhow, if I don't have but one shirt to my back – for I must tell you that some of my clothes are in Montgomery & I dont know when I can get them – The great reason is so hard to leave at present, is that it is impossible to tell when we may be ordered to perhaps up the Bigbee or Warrior. Selma, Montgomery or Mobile – So You see it would be hard for me to find my boat –

I write in haste & to let you know where I am at present – Will come & see you as soon a possible – for Oh! I do want to see you so much – I can't stand it much longer –

Yr Aff Son –
Carter Coupland

If you write to Demopolis -
Direct to care
Maj. T. M. LeBaron

- - - - -

Steamer *Dixie*
Demopolis Oct 18, 1864

My dear Mother

We are still in Demopolis awaiting orders from the QtrMasters; the Bigbee river is too low for us to go into, and I presume they will send us down the river to load with corn, and take around to Selma. I hope to get away tomorrow & if so it will take 4 or 5 days to reach Selma, which will be about next Saturday – the CSA's do business very slowly here – It has just commenced raining, for which I am sorry, as we may have to wait for a change in the river & proceed up instead of down. I hope you are well my darling Mother, often do I fancy you sick & lonely, and my heart yearns to be with you. Will this cruel war never end? – Oh, how happy I should be if I could only see you once a week; God grant the time may soon come.

I will come and see you as soon as possible –

Goodbye Yr Aff Son
Carter Coupland

- - - - -

Steamer *Prarie State*
Montgomery
November 28th 1864

My darling Mother –

Every day I go to the Post Office but am disappointed. I have only received two letters from you since I left Mobile, I write to you regularly every week & if you don't get my letters it is not my fault – I am uneasy dear Mother, fearful you are sick and perhaps in need; Oh! That I could but find the way that would afford me the means to make you comfortable, this is my great trouble on earth. Every thing looks gloomy – The merchants say they are all broke or will be, & there is no money or business in this portion of the Country – what is a poor man to do? Perhaps there may be better times in store for us; "Never give up" is my moto:

There is nothing definite regarding the sale of this Boat; the Govt has not yet given a decree, the Sale may be postponed until next term; if so, it will be six months off – however I cant say yet, we may yet get an order to sell in a few days.
Good bye dear Mother.
Yr Aff Son
Carter

- - - - -

Selma April 1st 1865

My dear Mother –

Arrived here yesterday – will leave this evening on Str "*Chero-kee*" for Montgomery – The "*Dixie*" sunk & Burnt on 24th Mch. Crew of [_ _ _] all Safe – I got your letters today. will answer them as soon as possible – I write this only to let you know I am Safe & well – Great excitement here today about Yankee Raids – I have not time to write more –

Good Bye my darling Mother,
Yr Aff Son Carter

114

(ed: This was the final Carter Coupland letter. There was a letter from Juliana Dorsey, his mother, to John R. Coupland, his brother, dated September 9, 1865. In the letter Juliana stated that, "Carter has lately married Maria Minse (?)" and that, "Carter . . . about the time of our surrender here (Meaning when Johnston surrendered to Sherman in late April, 1865) was on the Dixie, *she burnt and sunk and he barely escaped with his life, lost every article of clothing he had and for a fortnight was kept up the Coosa River, where he had been hiding cotton, and what he did for clothes cannot imagine – I have not seen him since Dec – he writes often, and aff – but cannot leave his business –"*

This was a September, 1865, letter discussing a March, 1865, sinking, and assuming Juliana was still with Cousin Tiff in Greensboro, then she referred to General Johnston's surrender in Durham and Greensboro and not the surrender at Appomattox on April 9, 1865.

Juliana's comment about seeing him in December, 1864, confirms that Carter did finally get a few days off from the boat and we presume visited her in Greensboro. Travel to Greensboro in late 1864 would have been very difficult. Many of the main railroads had been destroyed by Sherman's Union forces and lack of manpower and materials made repair of the railroads quite difficult.)

The Carter Coupland letters, Dorsey-Coupland Papers, 39.1 D73, Box 1, Folder 4, Special Collections Research Center, Swem Library, College of William & Mary, Williamsburg, Virginia.

Letters of the Davis and Sarah Wood Family
Botetourt County, Virginia

(ed: Davis Wood and Sarah Reynolds Wood lived on the southern edge of the town of Glen Wilton, Virginia. It is located less than 10 miles downstream from Clifton Forge, Virginia, which is the headwaters of the James River. The Wood farm was all river bottom land and included an island. The farm bordered the southern edge of Glen Wilton. Davis was primarily a farmer and also a Methodist preacher. The 1860 census reports showed Davis and Sarah with $12,000 of real property (land and buildings) and $15,000 of personal property which was mostly the value of their 26 Negroes. In 1860 their children were listed as: Sarah Elizabeth (15), James A. (13), Davis Miller (10), Lucy E. (8), George C. (5) and William E. (2). In August, 1861, Lelia Demarius will be born and in January, 1865, their last child, Robert Reynolds will be born. Sadly, in October of 1863, they will lose their oldest daughter, Sarah Elizabeth, to typhoid fever.

Davis attended Botetourt Seminary, was the valedictorian of his class, and the religious training is apparent in the 1864 and 1865 letters to his son. He had saved many of his handwritten sermons but a fire in the Wood family home in 1995 destroyed most of those documents.

Davis died in 1904 just 10 days shy of being 85 and Sarah died in 1910 about 40 days shy of being 87. Davis, who spent his life around horses, made a mistake in walking too close to the rear of a horse and got kicked in the chest causing internal injuries which resulted his death. Despite being born in a time when virtually every disease could kill you both he and Sarah lived long lives and those genes were passed to the children. With the exception of Sarah Elizabeth most of them lived into their 70's or beyond. George Corbin saw 83 years and James A. died at 92.) 1

- - - - -

[Letter from Sarah Reynolds Wood to her sister
Demarius Reynolds Pettyjohn]

Fall, 1861

My dear Mais,
I have received your last letter & glad to hear that you are well. Tho I cant write such good news from home, William has returned from his trip but is now in his bed very sick with Typhoid fever. Mr. Wood was up to see him. This morning he seemed a little better tho out of his head all night. Jennie nurses very well & she is his chief nurse. Corbin got home last Monday sick tho not confined to his bed yet. Ansalum Haden has been sick with Typhoid fever & mumps for some time 3 Doctors waiting on him but this evening he is dying. Mary has been sent for since dinner to see him die. Davis has been sent for to day to see Jimmie Circle who is very sick. Adam Shurman has also returned home from the Army sick, took cold with the measles & his recovery is doubtful.

Samuel Wood went out to Lewisburg to see if he could get his team he got 2 of his horses but could get no more, Mr. Wood can't get neither Waggon nor horses, & leaves us without horses to either ride or work. I don't know where to get any. Mr. Carper got back two of his horses, & what makes matters worse they wont put a wright value on the teams they keep, they only valued our Team at three hundred & forty dollars waggon & all, & some that were more valuable they valued less, they are hard cases. Cousin Joe Moore & his wife took supper with me yesterday eve they told me how the souldiers & waggoners treated people in their neighbourhood, ransack their houses, Take all the yarn, wool carpets. Kill their stock & destroy everything, burn & pull down the fences etc. Cousin Joe is entirely driven out from home & don't know when he can get back, have taken a great many things from them. Davis has gone to the Depot to day to see if he can get any thing for his Team. I expect he will bring news of another fight if the Cars are not two late coming in. Pa sent for Jimmie this evening to go to the Fork's for him on business. The old man does all he can, he stays with the hands pressing Tobacco but he looks broken down when he comes in the house, he needs some spirits to stimulate him but can't get any about here. I send him some when ever I can get it if you have any opportunity of sending him spirits do try and do it.

Bettie was up to see Will & Corbin this morning when she come I will hear how they are. Bettie & Nettie have just come. They say William is a little better tho out of his head all the time. he thinks he is at Suel Mountain yet he told Bettie to set on the bed by him, he asked if his toung was not very dry She said yes he said he was going to Boil it to right like the Devil, he talks all sort of foolishness night and day.

Dear Maiz I commenced this letter several days ago, but the river (James) was so high it could not be crossed, last Friday evening we had the most awful storm that the oldest men about here ever saw, I was afraid it would blow our house down, it blew off all

119

the top of that long barn old Brian built down to the logs tore it all to pieces, at Pas it blew up every persimmon tree & Locust tree by the roots, Mr. Wood had gone to the Depot it rained so that he could not get back, the first day & the next day it rained all day again so that he did not leave the depot till 6 oclock, by that time the river was in the road by the Forge so that he could scarcely pass, & trees had fallen through the Barrens that it was almost impassable, he did not know of the storm till he butted up against a large tree fallen across the road. It was so dark he had to get off his horse and feel for the road. I became so uneasy during the storm that I sent Jim to look for him Davis & the high water and trees fallen with the darkness put a stop to his journey & he came back with the news that he could not find him, all that kept me up was a faith in that God who can calm the storm and raging of the Sea.

Poor Ansalem Haden is buried today, at his Pas, with all the Honours of War men were sent for at the Depot; Corbin was not able to go he is quite unwell but not confined entirely to his bed, he looks very badly & said he has been getting weaker every day. William is very low, he is a little better today, he is not out of his head quite as much as he was a few days ago. have to sit up all night with him. I went to see him yesterday, he dont talk very much, looks very vacant out of his eyes. Poor Will you never saw him in such a fit on yesterday we thought his case was very doubtful but I hope he will mend now, as his tounge is improving. Jimmie Circle has sent for Mr. Wood today. to talk with him on the subject of Religion. he has been getting worse since I commenced this letter and now he is not expected to live. nearly every man that went out to Gauly River with their waggons are sick. I went up to see Corbin yesterday with Mr. Wood the children all go to see him, he sais he is very lonesome. Mary will return after her brother is buried she wanted to go home yesterday but could not cross the river.

George has just stopped in, and sais Aunt Mary is going on home. Ansalum was Mrs. Hadens favorite.

The high water has done us damage as well as the wind. The River run over the whole Island & our corn was under water but I hope we will save enough to bread us tho a great deal will be lost. Pougs Mill is entirely gone. Williams mill not injured that I know of I have never seen such distressing times in my life. The war going on, high water storms, and fear of loosing my brothers, is bad but still I feel that I ought not to complain, Gods will is all right – and things can yet be worse.

Pa & Mother keep up pretty well. Jennie complains a good deal, she sits up with William every night & waits on him through the day. I expect she will take a spell herself after the excitement is over. Miss Mary is still alive, Aunt Sallie is in bed sick she has had a dreadful cold. Mother looks well, but Pa seems to be troubled & fatigued but greater than you would expect. The scarlet Fever is at Major Paxtons & Mr. Rocks, but they are all getting well at Mr. Rocks. I haven't heard from the   lately. Dr. Walkup goes to see William every day, a horse will be sent to the River for him at 8 oclock this evening as the River can't be forded. I have not told you any thing about my health which I am glad to tell you is better than it has been for several years, I am very Nervous can't bear nois at all, the children annoy me dreadfully & I scold at them till I am ashamed of it – I can eat any thing and a big bare too don't suffer with Neuralzy but very little & can expose myself double to what I did before I went to the healing springs. that water is my cure all, I shall always have faith in the Healing Springs.

Oct 4th
Poor Jimmie Circle died last night and will be buried tomorrow at the Locust Bottom Grave Yard, the family are greatly distressed,

his wife waited on him with untiring Affection. I heard that Jimmie died happy, clapping his hands. O I scarcely ever felt so awful as I did this morning when I heard of the poor fellers death. his Parents were so devoted to him, would not let him got to War for fear he would get killed, but he got his sickness when he went to Gauly with his Waggon. & O Mais, we have come near looseing our dear Brother Will, but I am glad to tell you he is on the mend now, and we hope with proper attention, and the kindness of our maker he will recover. Corbin has been able to wride down to see William once this week tho he lookes worse than you ever saw him. The two Brothers cried when they met – Bettie has gone up to Pas this evening, she is devoted to her Uncle Will, he fondles on her so much when he is well, write ever your Ellen

If William gets worse I will write immediate, don't be uneasy. Lelia is the fattest little thing you ever saw & grows so fast. I wish you could see her.   2

(ed: William Reynolds, at age 33, died from Typhoid Fever on October 10, 1861. He was the favorite brother of both Sarah and Demarius. In the upcoming October 27 letter Sarah tells Demarius of William's passing. Demarius, age 27, would get Typhoid Fever and die a couple of months later.)

Reverend Davis M. Wood, circa 1875

Author's Collection

Obituary of William A. Reynolds by Reverend Davis Morton Wood:

Died at the residence of his father, Archelius Reynolds in Botetourt County, October 10th 1861 William A. Reynolds of Typhoid fever in the 34th year of his age.

He was the only one of a large family of children who remained at the old Homestead the hope of aged parents, for comfort and support in their declining years. He was a young man of promise for usefulness in society, amiable, courteous and kind, was generally loved and respected among his acquaintance. But in common with many others he had fallen victim to disease consequent upon exposure in the government transportation service in the western part of this State. He came home sick, was soon confined to his bed, with frequent spells of delirium, the disease rapidly assuming a severe and malignant type, terminating fatally in the course of three weeks.

Mysterious Providence! "The Lord gave, and the Lord has taken away, and blessed be the name of the Lord."   2

- - - - -

[Letter from Sarah Eleanor Reynolds Wood to her Sister Demarius Reynolds Pettyjohn:]

October 27 (1861)
My Dear Maiz

I received your letter yesterday evening, & your dissatisfaction in

124

not hearing from home as often as you wished to do, adds greatly to my already distressed feelings, instead of wilfully neglecting you I have been constantly thinking about you, and feeling the most heartfelt sympathy for you, how else would I feel to an only dearly loved Sister. I wrote to you as soon as we thought our dear Brother was seriously ill and the River [James] became so high that it was impossible to cross it in any way, & for some time after the water had fallen, it was reported the mail boy was drowned at all events, we had no mail for some time. I kept my letter and added to it til I could start it off, trying to give you all the news I could at the same time thinking William was improving in health, but suddenly the news came he was worse, & he died in two short a time to do anything, but just wait and see if he would not take a turn for the better, but no the finger of God was laid upon him. and we have to say, the will of the Lord be done. Our derly loved Brother is gone, & long will it be before the deeply wounded hearts will be healed, for our loss is a great one, never did a Sister enjoy the society of a Brother more than I did Williams, & espe-cially during the last Summer up to the time he went to Lewis-burg, we all seemed to be more attached to each other than usual, he came down here sometimes 2 and 3 times a week, & scarcely ever missed a Sunday but he was here, every child seemed to be glad & expect Uncle Will is coming & in such perfect Peace did we part for the last time, not one cross word has passed between us since I changed my name. O it does my heart good to think of the sweet intimacy that existed between us the Last day he spent on earth I stayed with him and comed his head he told me I did not know how much good it done him to come his hair & he talked to strong and raise himself up so well that I could scarce believe he was so near dying tho his pulse was sinking all the time. in the evening he held his hand and bid me farewell for the last time, the next morning he was a lifeless corps. Pa tried to bear up the best he could but sometimes would burst into tears like a child, but it seemed hard for Mother to give him up often through the day she would go and look at him. I saw her put her hand on his head and say O if he was only just asleep – just before he was carried out she took a last look at him and kissed him. Old Mr. Allen came in & she took him by the hand and said our all is gone. Pa and Mr. Allen both burst into tears when they met, - Our dear Brother was buried about a quarter of a mile from the house on the ridge back of the House the same place Pa picked out for himself. I will stop this distressing theme tho I know you want to hear all about it.

I was up to see mother today, she is mending thos quite feeble yet. she sits up by the fire til she gets tired, and then layes down a while, & so on through the day, Corbin is mending slowly. Davis has been sitting up with him and goes to see him regular. Corbin was very low a few days ago, he took a changed for the better or he would have been dead before now. & he is not entirely out of danger yet. no more cases of fever (Typhoid) have oc-curred in the family since. I forgot to tell you the reason I did not write after Jennie, she wrote in my place & we all was so sure you would come right away that I thought it useless to write, we looked for you till I received your letter yesterday evening, Jennie even cleaned up her room upstairs for you, Saturday.   2

(ed: The first daughter, and also the first child, of Reverend Davis M. Wood and Sarah Eleanor Reynolds Wood would die on October 2, 1863. Sarah Elizabeth 'Bettie' Wood was born on October 20, 1845, and was almost 18 years of age when she passed. The most likely cause of death was Typhoid Fever. She was buried in the Wood family cemetery near Glen Wilton, Virginia.)

(ed: The oldest son of Davis and Sarah was James A. Wood. In the late summer of 1863 the Botetourt Home Guard was formed and James A. Wood (age 16) was part of the Dagger Springs Company which was mostly from the Glen Wilton area. The Home Guard was formed to provide local protection. The commands were composed of boys too young for service and men that were either too old or had an exemption.

James A. enlisted in Confederate Army on April 23, 1864, slightly ahead of the September date, when at age 17, enlistment would have been required. By enlisting early he was able to get a cash bonus for himself and a furlough for George Carper, a neighbor and messmate of his, in Co. D of the 11th Virginia Infantry. Private Wood joined Co. D on the Cold Harbor battlefield, near Richmond, in early June.

In the following letter Davis writes at length about boxes of foodstuffs sent to James and also one to the Carpers. These articles from home were very important to the underfed soldiers. He also tells James that he has a new brother, Robert Reynolds Wood, who was born on January 19th. In the paragraph on family information he covers who is sick both in the family and among the servants (slaves) and then Davis speaks of local unmarried women having babies and one young "Miss" who put her baby "in a hollow log, where it was found dead."

Late in the letter Davis wrote of his hopes for a "Foreign Power" to recognize the Confederacy so that Lincoln would only be President of the Northern States.)

[Letter from Reverend Davis M. Wood to his son Private
James A. Wood:]

Pleasant Hill, Botetourt, Va
February 5th 1865
My Dear James;

Your Uncle Corban has returned safe and sound. He reported that
you and your companions were all quite well, which you may
be sure, gave us much pleasure. But we were very sorry to hear
that your Box had failed to come to hand. I hope, however, that
you have received it and feasted on its contents. If you have not
received it, I presume it has been detained at the junction, where, I
learn things frequently lie over for some time. It would be well to
get a detail from your mess to see after the Boxes – one directed
to you, and the other to the Carpers – or through your Captain,
communicate with some of the R. Road Officials to inquire after,
and forward your Boxes. You have in your Box two letters, a pair
of gloves with fur gauntlets, two splendid pair of socks, 2 Turkies,
7 chickens, 1 ham of Pork, 2 Cakes of butter, 1 Sponge Cake, a
number of pies, sweet cakes, and biscuits, a few irish potatoes,
and apples, dried peaches and apples, beans and meal, tallow and
soap, lard to fry chicken, and a small tin cup. Quite a variety and
too valuable to lose without some effort to secure them.

Perhaps you will be surprised to hear that you have another Brother – a fine large baby – and as Wash said to Bill the next morning
after he was born, "Gentlemen, I tellyou that's much man in the
house." A good many say he favors you. He was born on the 19th
of January, the next day after Uncle Corban left for Richmond.

Your Ma has had a bad cold and cough, but is now improving, and
will be well in a few days. The children are generally well. Lucy

Sarah Eleanor Reynolds Wood and young Robert, circa 1870-1872

Author's collection

is our housekeeper now – she sends her love to you. Lelia is as lively as ever and often talks about Bro Jimmie. Georgie and Willie have been spending several days with their Grand Ma. Davis has had quite a time with the Confederate, but is now about well. They are well at your Grand Ma's. Your Cousin Saml Wood has been right sick for several days. I was to see him this evening. He thinks that he is a little better, able to walk and sit up at the fire. The rest are well. Our servants Are generally well. Kit has come home with a daughter. Ruth had a boy the 2nd instant. Babies are plenty up this way. Miss Bettie Lemon is said to have a daughter and a Miss Gilleland, on Cowpasture, had a baby and is reported to have put it in a hollow log, where it was found dead – and a Miss, on Jackson's River is said to be expecting! What a state of things.

Miss Jane Ann, Ida, & Bell Circle were to see your Ma this day week. They were well. I saw the Miss Carpers today all well. Adam Buhrman escorted them from Church. He is home furloughed – assigned to light duty – looking very well. No neighborhood news afloat of special interest.

Many are in hopes of peace. But for my part I do not confide in Yankee sincerity, and would not be surprised if they are not trying to lull our people into _____ _____ _____ ____ ___
___ _____ ____ _____ _____ in the Spring Campaign. I hope however that our officials will be wide awake and our soldiers too. Dont have anything to do with their trashy papers – "Yankee Notions" – and such like – they are corrupt in style and moral and unfit for a Southern Man to read. Now is the time for Soldiers to hold up their heads – and not talk despondingly. There is undoubtedly a pressure upon the Yanks of somekind, either from other Nations, or among themselves, and it seems only necessary for us to endure bravely a few months longer and our independence will be recognised by Foreign Powers. It is my hope, that after

the 4th of March Lincoln will be only considered <u>President</u> of the <u>Northern States</u>.

May God in his Mercy & good pleasure grant us Peace. – This we must <u>Pray</u> for, <u>hope</u> for, and <u>fight</u> for. The Lord bless & save you my son. Your ever affectionate Father

D. M. Wood

write soon and let us know about you box whether all was safe. I put hickory strips around each end of your box so that there would be a little trouble to get in. All join in much love to you. Remember me to the boys and tell them to keep in good heart. There are some nice girls at Home yet who will welcome them home when the war is over. Many of them say they would rather marry a brave soldier, who had lost a leg or an arm in defense of his country than the shirking money-grabbing cowards who remain at home and try to ruin poor girls, as some do, and have done.

<u>All</u> <u>honor</u> the <u>Brave</u> <u>Soldier</u>.   3

(ed: Davis must have felt a little guilty telling James all the details of young women who had gotten pregnant and had babies out of wedlock. In his margin notes he attempts to reassure the men that plenty of "nice girls" remain to marry them when the war is over.

The 11th Virginia was manning the "Howlett Line" in the Bermuda Hundred section of the Confederate trenches near Chester and Petersburg, Virginia. The Confederate defensive line of trenches stretch from north of Richmond to south

131

and west of Petersburg. The 11th Virginia was mostly in-
volved in picket duty and manning the line of trenches. They
had been defending this sector of the line since the early fall
of 1864.)

- - - - -

[Letter from Private James A. Wood to his mother
Sarah E. R. Wood:]

Camp near R[ichmond]

My dearest Mother

I sit down again after waiting patiently for a week to hear from
you all but I have not gotten on yet I suppose you all have forgotten me or you would write oftener. Since I _____ _____
_____ _____ mail call _____ from home. I got one
from Cousin _____ yesterday also one from Mr. Brooke to
day he rather surprised me for although you spoke in your last letter of his promising you to write to me I did not expect to get one
quite so soon. He wrote a very kind letter to me indeed & seem to
have a sage hand as he wrote well all well he spoke of being at our
house on the _____ of corn & said he did not know what would
become of him if it was not for our island. He gave me some very
good advice for which I am very thankful. I want to answer it as
soon as I can but feel a ___reacy about it for you know how fool-
ish I am about writing anyhow especially to Mr. Brooke as he is
anyhow especially to Mr. Brooke as he is
RICHMOND
very particular you know I hardly know what I am to do about it
as I am such a bold hand to write a letter – you must not look for

132

anything interesting from me as everything is so dry down here we hardly hear anything. _____ _____write often and write a long letter for you have a better chance than I have.

I hope you will not make yourself so uneasy about me for I have a very good time down here only on picket. But then we are there only a day & night. Tell Davis he might write often and give me details of his adventures during his hunting life. Tell him that Tom P says that he must write to him As I have no more time to write. I write so that I hope this will find you all as well as this leaves me   give my love to all my friends & take a good share for your dear self. God keep you all in his holy keeping is the prayer of your devoted son.

Jimmie

PS Tom sends his respects to you all   excuse mistakes   3

(ed: This letter was in the worst condition of the entire group and portions were impossible to read. The large "RICHMOND" was at the bottom of page 1. The Davis in the last paragraph was his younger brother, who is 14, and not his father Reverend Davis M. Wood. He would address him as father and not by his first name. Tom P was Private Tom F. Perkins who enlisted in Co. D of the 11th. Virginia Infantry on June 15, 1864, and was a neighbor from the Glen Wilton area.

The next letter, dated February 26th from Bermuda Hundred, covers a variety of subjects but by far the most important is the question of "negros in the army" and the remarkable view of a 17 year old private. He also writes of disease at home, a possible exchange of prisoners, some brotherly advice on keeping the horses safe, and the cash bonus he got for enlisting early and the furlough that George Carper, his messmate, earned for bringing him in early.)

- - - - -

[Letter from Private James A. Wood to his mother Sarah E. R. Wood:]

Camp near Bermuda Hundred
February 26, 1865

My Dear Mother

I sit down this Sabbath morning to write you a few lines your welcome letter has just come _____ to hand and carefully perused. We have moved from the river and comeback to our old camp where the Tar Heels were camped in our places. They burned our houses down seven in the company ours included but we got into another until we can rebuild. you spoke of a fight near Richmond I suppose it was at Hatchers Run it wasn't near us. I am sorry to hear that the soldiers are doing so badly but that's this war I think Pa had better not let his corn go too fast or he will not have enough to do him he had better put some in a safer place than the corn crib & they will not be so apt to find it but I hope they will not pester you any more. I know the soldiers fare badly enough but there is no use in doing so badly & no body that thought much of himself would do so. – I am sorry to hear that the dyptheria is at Mr. Biggs. I hope he has not lost anyone else did any of the white family die? I think he had better send for Dr. Neal & not be at outs with him at such a time.

There is no news stirring now ther was eciteyment in camp the other day about the negro question. every man in camp but 4 or 5 voted for putting them in. I think that it looks rather strange for us to do the samething that we were so much against at the first of the war. it looks like a drowning man catching at a straw. And if we should put the negros in the army & by that means should gain our independence why they & not us would get the credit. then they could say that they fought for & gained the independence of the South. We have been against freeing the negroes against abolishinism & now we turn around & do that same thing because we are in (some think) rather a tight place. admit that we are. did we not say that we were fighting in a just cause & thus God was on the side of the south. Then why cant we say so still & put our trust in God who is the God of battles who can win with us (without the aid of the negroes) as an instrument drive the yankes not only from our country but clear out of existence. well enough about the Yanks

I received a letter from Coz Nettie Fryday they are well with the exception of colds she is teaching school & is very well pleased down there says they are well at Uncle Isaacs Coz Mary Rucker sent me a Christian paper the other day, she marked a piece heading the parting words to her soldier son probably you have seen it before – she says that Sammie is well & that she expects him to be exchanged soon as there will probably be a general exchange of prisoners. I hope there will be – I am glad to hear that the little miss is growing so fast and doing well. I reckon Tillie is as pretty as ever & quite as mischevious I expect a little quiter as to be. – Tell Davis that he must make haste & answer my letter & keep the horses close or some of those soldiers might accidentally make a mistake & ride one of them off. Tell him to keep a good door & lock to the stables.

I suppose George C has been up to see you before this as he has gotten home just in time I suppose to get the benefit of the snow he got a furlough on me as a recruit I would have gotten half of it but there was an order against that. I had to put up with $275 & stay here I could have gotton more that that but as George is one of my neighbors & messmates & therefore I could not be hard with him & it is not in accordance with my nature to be hard with anyone. They have suspended the furlough business with the exception of us in the Hundred. It is probable that they will continue that way all year. I guess I will not get a furlough soon unless I get sick, but I hope there will be no need of furlough much longer for I hope that there will soon be peace but then the Yankess say there shall be no peace.

I must stop, write soon & a long letter to your ever loving son

Jimmie 2

(ed: In December, 1863, Mr. Archelius Reynolds passed away. His last will and testament was dated March 11, 1862, and was probated in Botetourt County, Virginia, in February, 1864. He named both his son Corbin Reynolds and his son-in-law Davis M. Wood as the executors of his estate. Corbin withdrew and Davis served as the executor for the estate.

The personal property of the estate is to be sold after making arrangements for "ample funds for the comfortable and decent maintenance" of his wife, Sarah E. Reynolds. The total amounted to some $7234 of appraised value based on pre-war prices. Sixteen slaves accounted for $5000 of the total. Because of the continued inflation of Confederate cur-

rency and the very real prospect of the war soon ending and slaves being free there was virtually no market for the sale of slaves. The appraisal of property had been done in April of 1864, and now almost a year later, Davis had made no move to attempt to sell the slaves. George W. Pettyjohn, Sr. writes Davis, in the upcoming letter, acting for his wife Nancy Reynolds, and demands that he sell the slaves.)

- - - - -

[Letter to Davis M. Wood from Mr. George W. Pettyjohn, Sr. of Amherst Cty., Virginia:]

Lynchburg Va   March the 20th 1865

Mr. Davis M. Wood

Dear Sir

I have understood that you have postponed the sale of the Negroes, horses, & mule of the late Archelus Reynolds deced. untile next fall; oweing to there being no bidders for negroes in that section of country; now all that I have to say in the matter is, that the negroes, horses, & mule should be brot to Lynchburg & put up at auction to the highest bidder for money & let the property be sold & each Legatee have there share at once & each Legatee bare there proportionable parts in fetching the property to market; whear there will be plenty of bidders; you speak in your letter, that there are many Yankeys traverseing your Country; now you will see that those negroes may be taken by them; or they may go off

137

to the Yankeys & then all will be lost; I am acting for my wife & if they should go off or be taken by the Yankeys I shall hold you as the Executor, or administrator responsible for my wifes portion; as this property should have been sold over twelve months ago.

Yours Very Respectfully

Geo W Pettyjohn Sr   2

(ed: Davis M. Wood never sold the slaves. In January of 1865 he had sold the cows, calves, and yearlings. The balance of the personal property was sold at auction in November of 1865. On the date that Mr. Pettyjohn writes his letter General Lee is just 3 weeks away from surrendering his army to General Grant.

There was no record indicating why Davis chose never to take any of the slaves to market. It could have simply been that they were needed to continue the work of running the Reynolds farm. In 1864 Davis may have still hoped for a Confederate victory and didn't want the double impact of losing the farm workforce and selling the slaves below market appraised value. March was now time to think about spring planting and slaves would bring virtually nothing on the market with the Confederacy on the brink of defeat.)

(ed: All of the above mentioned estate sales to liquidate the property of Archelius Reynolds are recorded in the Botetourt County records at the Court House in Fincastle, Virginia. A full accounting of items, quantities and prices can also be found in No Soap, No Pay, Diarrhea, Dysentery & Desertion.)

(ed: On April 6, 1865, both Sarah and Davis wrote their son a letter. As they posted their letter the 11th Virginia Infantry was being defeated and James A. was being captured at Sayler's Creek. The entire Confederate army was retreating westward and surrender at Appomattox Courthouse was only 3 days away.)

- - - - -

[Letters from Sarah E. R. Wood and Davis M. Wood to their son Private James A. Wood:]

Pleasant Hill Botetourt Va
April 6, 1865

My dear Jimmie

Your truely welcome letter of the 28th. ultimo came last night to relieve me of uneasiness that none but a Mother can feel, we heard that Pickets division was sertainly in a late fight - & my imagination would occasionally run over the dark side of the picture, and see you dead or wounded. but not withstanding that, I had a kind of faith that all was well with you, which proved to be true. but how long such good luck will last is fearfully unsertain with me. but I will commend you to care of him who careeth for you, & has great pitty for me. It is very distressing to me to know that you have to undergo so many hardships & privations, and sometimes whilst I have so many table comforts set before me, I think of our dear absent son and silently grieve that he is not here to partake of our enjoyment.

139

This is truely a cruel war and I feel more on the subject now than ever. It is awful to read how our Southern people are treated by the Yankies. Lately turning poor women & children out doors to starve. I hope God will punish them as they deserve, we are well at present – tho this damp weather keeps me complaining. We have had so much rain & high water that little can be done towards makeing another crop or gardening. The river can scarcely ever be forded. Your Pa had to go round by the Brige yesterday to the Post-O & the shoe makers shop, Davis went over to Daniel Latins to get his pistol fixed he got back this evening & bought a carbine with him which he gave 50 dollars for. Tis a very nice little gun, he has been out & killed a squirl with it, this evening. Davis has grown so much since you left, he has gone to regular ploughing, but if our teacher come he will stop farming, I am getting very fearful this war will continue till the Poor feller will have to leave home as you have done, and that will add trouble to trouble.

I hav'nt much news to tell you, Charlie Circle has turned the corner and is now considered our enemy, Bell was here a few evenings ago, she enquired after you & said Robert favoured you. I suppose you will expect to see a little likeness of yourself when you come home, he is a great big fat feller. All are well at Mothers the Old Lady eat Turkey with us Monday She seemed to be very uneasy about you since the fighting. I understand that Henry Wood and George Dearing are going to Buchanan to live . . . . . Comisary department, Dearing belonged to Jacksons command at the time Henry did. he must be pleased with Ann E – he goes there about once a week & some times stays two or thre days, he has an easy birth compared with the rest of our soldiers. Miss Susan Booze is weaving for me she the best weaver I ever had, & real old hand to work every way. I hav'nt heard from Amherst lately, Sue is getting along finely she stays at Corbins a good deal of her time. Corbin and Daniel Circle had falling out Lately about

140

the gails that washed on Daniels fields, he & old W Circle dont get along atall Daniel curses his Father and threatens to shoot his Negroes, As your Pa wants to write some I will stop, give my best regards to Tom P. Always tell me when you get my letters, write very soon and often

to your loving Mother
S. R. Wood

What do you think of our Union friends in Amherst? They have sertainly gone asstray

- - - - -

My Dear Jimmie; As the Spring Campaign has now opened, you may well immagine our anxious solicitude for your welfare. We heard various rumors of your Division – one that you had come to Highbridge – another that you had gone to Wytheville – another to North Carolina, and last, that you were in the big fight at Petersburg. We saw in the papers that Genl. Terry had been wounded and we supposed he was your Genl. But we have since learned it was not your Genl. We were thankful to Our Heavenly Father to hear from yourself of your welfare. And we cease not to commend you, night and morning, to God and his Grace. And I hope my son you will remember, and feel your dependence upon God, at all times, but especially when upon the battlefield with death dealing bullets falling thick and fast around you, and fellow Soldiers falling wounded and dead! Then to whom can we look but God! He alone can deliver. He can, and I hope will, send a guardian Angel to be with you by day and by night. Put your trust in God. And as I have said to you before, so I say again, do nothing to forfeit the favor of God. Do not cherish wicked feeling and

141

opinions. Remember the Lord's prayer – "forgive as I forgive" and though you are a soldier, confronting an enemy, yet you must do so from principle _____ matter of duty to your country, and not form a spirit of malice, or of revenge, and always be ready to be kind and human when your enemy is in your power. But always be watchful of Yankees. Never be too ready to confide in them. They are generally not to be trusted.

Have nothing to do with Gambling, and drinking Spirits – except as a medicine – Take not the Sacred Name of God in vain. Read your Testament at all leisure times, and pray the Holy Spirit to enlighten your mind and enable you to comprehend his truth aright. Christ is your Savior. He died for you. His blood atones for sin – for the sins of the world – so that every one who repents of sin – is truly sorry for his sins, hates, and forsakes them, and trust in Christ, is forgiven. God is pledged to forgive such, and to cleanse from all unrighteousness. The Lord help you by his grace to repent and trust in Christ to the saving of your soul. Pray much and pray earnestly, and believingly. If ever you had occasion to be serious and in earnest about your soul, you surely have now a most urgent need. Death rides on every paping breeze. How solemn should you feel. "A point of time, a moments space Removes you to your heavenly place, Or shuts you up in Hell." O my son, I feel very solicitous for your welfare, both now and hereafter. And if it should be the will of God to permit you to fall in battle, it would be a great satisfaction to hear of your faith and hope in Christ. God bless you my son, and save you for Christ's sake, Amen. your loving Father, Davis M. Wood

We have heard that your Captain was missing or killed. From this we infer that you have . . . [rest of letter missing]   3

142

(ed: The notes that were shown after the signatures of Sarah and Davis were written in the margins. The remaining words written by Davis were so faded that they were impossible to read. As you read the above letter there can be little doubt that Davis preaches sermons at the Glen Wilton Methodist Church.

The final letter in the grouping was dated April 9, 1865. As Davis writes his letter the Army of Northern Virginia was being surrendered to the Army of the Potomac at Appomattox Courthouse. The war in Virginia was over. Private James A. Wood was enroute to a Union prison camp in Newport News, Virginia.

Davis still had high hopes for the Confederacy or perhaps he was just trying to boost his son's spirits. The Confederacy was lost but Davis and Sarah Wood had won because their son, James, had survived and the war has ended before their next son, Davis, was called into the army.)

- - - - -

[Letter from Davis M. Wood to his son
James A. Wood:]

Sunday Evening Home
April 9th 1865

My Dear James;

We were disappointed in sending to the office several days ago, and I suppose it was well enough, as events have transpired which make it very probable that this letter would have fallen into the hands of the Yankees. We have heard of the evacuation of Richmond. This was no doubt a stroke of policy on the part of Genl Lee for the purpose of concentrating his forces, and drawing the Yankees farther from their base of supplies. The Campaign is now about to be an active one, instead of the slow tedious one of siege, as was the case of Richmond. Get the Yankees away from their Gunboats, and entrenchments then will come the tug of war. And then, with the blessings of God, success will be ours.

There are some weak-kneed people, and soldiers too; But that has been the case in all wars, in all countries, in every age of the world. On such people and soldiers there can be no reliance in this our great struggle. They are ready to jump to either side as it may be successful. Such are not loyal to their Country, nor true to great principles, such as are involved in this our great struggle for independence and nationality. The Negro is only a pretext and a fanatical hobby on the part of the Yankees. States rights, or the exclusive control of a sovereign state over its own domestic, internal institutions, without the dictation of other States through their representatives in Congress, yes This right was guaranteed by the old Constitution, and original compact of Union, of the old United States is the great principle for which we contend and for this we are willing to sacrafice Negro slavery, rather than become slaves to the Yankees. Had they been actuated by feelings of philanthrophy for the Negro, how easy it would have been to purchase their freedom. But no, they prefer to spend money to destroy their white brethren, possess the lands they never cleared, and houses they never built. Who can believe that God will permit the Yankees to succeed! I still hope for final success to the Confederacy. God bless you my son. Amen
D. M. Wood

in a fight. If you are safe, as I hope you are, be thankful to God, and trust him son.

As to the employment of Negroes as soldiers in our army, I think this ought to have been done long ago. I would sooner rely on faithful Negroes than weak-kneed whites. I would like to hear how our Negroes have behaved in Lee's army. If you come in reach of Genl Hoke's division inquire for Rucker, he is a medical teamster.   3

(ed: James A. Wood was released from prison on July 1, 1865, after taking the 'Oath of Allegiance.' He returned to Glen Wilton and became a farmer. He married Sabina Payne on March 25, 1872, and they had 10 children. James died in 1938 at the age of 92 and is buried in the cemetery on the property of the Locust Bottom Presbyterian Church.)

1.   1860 U. S. Census Reports, Provo, UT, Ancestry.com, M653-1336, P. 342; 1860 Slave Census for Botetourt County, Virginia.

2.   Patte Wood, "The Family History of Joseph Wood & Mary Epperson Wood of Botetourt County," 3 July 1995, private printing; Jeff Toalson, "They Will Think I Am Crazy, But I Am Not," 1996, private printing, p21 – P43.

3.   Original letters in the author's personal collection.

Sabina Payne Wood and James A. Wood, circa 1880

Author's collection

"I still remain your loveing wife untill death"
The letters of Mrs. Josephine Robison of Maury County, Tennessee

(ed: Letters from the women at home, whether wives, sisters, mothers or sweetheart, are the rarest items in literature of the conflict. Women's letters went to the front and usually ended up being used for campfires or toilet paper. They seldom made it back home. Because of that the surviving letters of women are quite valuable and in many ways are of greater value than the letters of the soldier. Only four of Josephine Robison's letters to her husband, John W. Robison, are known to have survived.

Josephine had a unique and powerful writing style. These four letters will make you wish that there were additional examples of her voice that had survived. I am regularly visited by many of her thoughts but especially her lament to John that, "I think sometimes that I have not got a friende on earth . . . I never ly down at night but wat I think where is my loved one tonight.")

- - - - -

Maury County, Tennessee
February the 13, 1862

Dear beloved husban,

This is to let you know that I received a letter from you tonight whitch give me mutch plesure to here from you that you was well.

But oh what news I have herde tonight I have herde that you have all lefte where you was and had gon to Fourte Donelson and I am so uneasy about you. Your Father brought me the letter and tolde me that you wall all gon. He see Mur[ra]y Lockharte today and he tolde him about it. I am sorry to here that you have lefte where you was for I thought maby I would get to come and see you, but it has happen that I can not come and see you but I hope it is all for the better. Wee know not what it is for but our God above knows – yes He knows more than wee do. If wee never meete on this earth agan I hope we will meete where parting will be no more. I trust in heven wee bouth shall rain – I trust in heven wee will meete again.

John, I started a letter to you laste Wednesday. I rote in it about coming to see you. I do not know whether you will get it or not. I want you to right to me whether you get it or not.

I got a letter from Hannah the other day. She is well. Your Father's folks is all well. They got a letter from Will las Fryday. He is well and one from you Mother. She has not bin well for some time. John when you mother rights to you I want you to right to me about it.

John I have herde that Eli is at the place whare you have gon to. Ifen he is tell him I sed howdy to him and Uncle to and tell them I would be glad to see them bouth and tell Cooper howdy for me and tell him I would like to see him to and all of the reste of my friends.

John you sed you wanted to know whether I rote that letter for Becky to Harve to not. I did right it for her.

John, I love you yes I do. Oh how sad and how gloomy the hours

I am lefte alone to study over the paste hours that has gon by that we never can call back. Oh how bad I uste to hate to see you go of and leve me a few hours of a Sunday but if you was here now it looks like I could not mind a few hours but now I have to give you up one long yere. Oh the time seems so long to me. It seems like it has bin a yere since you wente away. Ifen I just knowed you would live to git back when your time is out I could contente my self better. I sed one long yere but it mabe as long as life last but Oh I hope and pray to God that it will not be as long as one yere for I do want to see you so bad. I cannot work today for studying about you. I think maby I ma be here well and not in no danger, and you ma be away of her, ded or wounded. Oh how bad it makes me feel when I think of it.

Will ses when his time is out he is acoming home. I want to see him mighty bad but I routher see you acoming than him. John I wish you could see yore little children. Sister can walk all over the house and is as fat as a little pig. She has got five teeth. You sed you wanted to know whether she suckes or not. Yes she dose an can say titty as good as I can. You sed you wanted me to kiss them bouth for you. I do hug and kiss them every day for you. Tomy is the same olde Tom.

John wee have not got the meessels yet and they have bin all round us. Winney folks has had them and Les folks is got them and Mister Skelley folks and Mister Mekees folks.

So nothing more at present. I still remain your loveing wife untill death. So fare you well for every more.

> I have loste my mate – my trubels grate
> And now I am lefte alone.
> No one can tell the greefe I feel
> Now simphythise my friende.

149

Remember me when this you see – Though many miles aparte we be.

Josey

(ed: John and the entire Maury Light Artillery were captured, at Fort Donelson, on February 16, 1862. They were shipped via riverboat and railroad to Camp Douglas, Chicago, Illinois, as prisoners of war. They would remain prisoners for almost 7 months. John's letters from Camp Douglas were very vanilla and contain no information about prison life. We can only assume that all prison letters were censored.)

- - - - -

Maury Cnty., Tennessee
July the 18, 1862

Dear Beloved Husban,

I again take my seete to drop you a few lines to let you know that Father and me receive your too last letters whitch give us mutch pleasure to here that you was in good health and injoying yourself. This leaves us all well but Sis. She has had a sevear rising on one of her little breste but it is getting better now. Her and Tomy both has bin afflicted with risings. Tomy hade one on his knee about a month ago. It was so bad I begin to think it would make a cripple of him but it has got sound and well now. I hope when these few lines comes to your hande they ma find you in good health.

I have nothing strange to right. John you don't talk like you think you will be at home shortly. I do want to see you so bad I don't know wat to do. Some times I think I will see you before long and then again I get out of harte and think I never will be seeing you enymore, but I try to live in hopes, if I dy in despair. I do hope and trus and pray to God ever day for your return to me and your little children.

I hope you are treated well [in Camp Douglas Prison] and I hope those that you thought was your enamyes is your friends. John there is none thing in your laste letter that if I knowed you mente it the way that I take it I could shout for joy and prase my Lorde for granting my prayers that I have prayed to Him from the bottom of my harte. O John I think it is harde that wee cannot get to see etch other. I do hope that God ma put an ende to this war some way so He letes the people live. You sed you wanted me to right to you where Hannah is. She is at the asylum yet I rote to here what you sed in your letter. Farther is going to starte to Nashville tomorrow and I am going up that way and stay until he comes back. He will go to see Hannah.

John I want you to right to me how you are off for close. [how well off you are for clothes] Whether you have got eny are not. I do not know what you will do this winter for close if you have to stay there. Your Father's folks is all well. They have not herde from your Mother in a longe time. If she has forgot that she had one I have not forgot how I have one. I know I have got one as lovely as the blooming flowers in the month of June.

The helth of the neighborhood is good. Tell all the boys that went from about here that thare folks and fameless is all well. Father's family is well. So nothing more. I must quit and go to bed for it is geting late. Right soon as you get this.

Josie

(ed: Hannah Trotter, Josephine's sister, was employed by the Insane Asylum in Nashville, Tennessee. Mr. Trotter carried Josie's letter to Nashville and Hannah wrote a short letter, on July 21st., that was included in the same envelope.

John would not have to spend another winter in Camp Douglas. He would be shipped to Vicksburg, Mississippi, for exchange, in early September and was exchanged on October 20, 1862.)

- - - - -

Maury Cty, Tennessee
March the 3, 1863

My dear beloved husban,

I take my pen in han to drop you a few lines to let you know that wee are all well an I do hope when those few lines comes to your hand they may finde you enjoying the same blessings.

John I have no news mutch to right to you more than wee have see a heepe of soldiers for the laste too weeks. Whitfield's Division paste through Santa Fee laste Fryday. They campt over in them woods between here and the Widdow Joneses a few days. They was Texasans. You aught to seen us all waved our handkercheefs at them.

John youre Father is going to leeve us. I do knot know what will become of me and your little children for he is all that I have to

152

look to for ascistance but I will try and do the best I can. Oh that you was with me tonight. I think sometimes that I have not got a friende on earth. Oh John I do wante to see you so bad. I love you better than I every did in my life. I know what it is to give up the nereste bosome friend that I had on earth. My mind is never off of you. You are the las thing that is on my mind when I ly down on my resting pillow at night and the first thing that is on my mind when I wake from my slumber and you are often with me in my dreams. I never ly down at night but wat I think where is my loved one tonight. Is he standing somewhere chille with colde are is he lying on the colde ground thinly covered are is he lying some wher on the battle field cold and deathless are wher so can he be so fare from his bosome friend tonight? Oh if wee never meete on this earth again, ma wee meete in heaven wher parting will be no more.

You sed for me to let you know whether I neede any money or not. I will not stande in neede of eny for a while. If you draw eny and do not neede it yourself and can get any chance to sende it to me you can sende it.

Nily and Mit is here tonight to stay with there Father the las night. Mit ses tell you that she has not forgotten you but it looks like you have forgot her. She ses right to her. Nily ses she would have rote to you but she had no paper. They all sende there best love to you. Give Cooper my beste love and Brant Harbison if he is thare and all the reste of my friends.

I will remain your loving wife untill death.

Josie

Tomy send howdy to you.

(ed: John's father had joined the Confederate army as a substitute, for Mr. Tim Chappell, to pay off a personal loan. In effect he was hired as the substitute for the amount he owed. John was working with Captain Sparkman to get him transferred to the Maury Light Artillery because he does not think his father could stand the hardships of being a private in the army. This left Josie without family support in 'Santa Fee'.)

(ed: John and the Maury Light Artillery (sometimes referred to as Sparkman's Battery – 1st Tennessee Artillery) were part of the garrison defending Port Hudson, Louisiana. Vicksburg and Port Hudson were the last two Confederate fortifications blocking the Mississippi.)

- - - - -

Santa Fee, Tennessee
June 20, 1863

My hearte and hand

My dear beloved husban

I take my seete one time more to drope you a few lines in anser to your kind letter whitch I received a few days ago barin date May the 16 whitch give me grate sattisfaction to heare from you for it looked like it had bin a long time since I had got one from you. I had almost got out of hearte of ever getting another one from you and I want to here from you just as bad now as I did before I got

154

the last letter for I have herde since that they had a very harde fight down there.

Oh how unhappy it renders me to think whilst I am righting, your preshes and lovely form ma be lying under the silent duste. What an aking hearte I have this lone and sad evening. To think that I am righting to one that I love better than everthing else on this earth and cannot never, no never get to gaze on your sweete smiling face.

Oh how happy I was las night in my dream. I drempe that you come home. I thought that you slipt up and no one knowed that you was on the place untill you slipt in at the door. I thought when I first saw your face I could not move for a while and then I thought I sprang up and flew to you and took you in my arms. Oh don't you know that I was glad in my sleep and I thought that your sweete little babe went to you and put her arms around your neck and huged you.

We are all well and I do hope when those few lines comes to your hand they may find you in good health. I wish you could all get to come home and stay at home with the ones that loved you beste. Tomy ses he wishes you could come home. He ses he wants to see his pa.

You wanted to know whether I need eny money are not. I do not neede eny now. I hav drawed twenty dollars sence your Father went away and I have not spente eny of the mony that your Father give me, yet I do not knough when I will neede eny. I will right to you when I neede eny. I herde yesterday that soldier's wifes could sende to Columbia and draw a half bushel of salt. That will helpe me out mightly. I have got a sow and six very nice shoats. I want to try to make my meete out of them nexte year.

So I will bring my lines to a close by asking you to right soon. I rote a letter las Sunday was a week ago to send by Smith and he did not com an get them.

Tell you Father and Cooper howdy for me. I was sorrow to here that Cooper was sick be we all have to be sick and we all have to dy. So fare you well my deareste dear. I will bid you adew. My hearte is all moste broke and I would be glad to see you.

Josie

- - - - -

(ed: Port Hudson was captured by Federal forces on July 9, 1863. John was paroled on July 12, 1863, and he returned to Maury County, Tennessee. The Maury Light Artillery would not be reformed and John would not serve with any other Confederate units during the remaining two years of the war. When John got home to Josie, their little son William Thomas ('Tomy') is 5 and Mary Angeline Eugenia ('Sissy') is 3.)

(ed: John and Josephine had additional children. Eliza T. was born in 1865, James W. in 1866, Sallie E. in 1869, and John G. in 1873. John died on July 13, 1900, in Memphis. Josephine passed away in 1932.)

The John W. Robison Letters, Brewer Library, United Daughters of the Confederacy, Richmond, Virginia.

Postscript

Perspective is so easy to lose when considering events that happened in the past. It is difficult to view past events without injecting some presumption of moral authority. For some reason we tend to judge past actions based on current standards. We need to view history in the context of time and not judge by standards of a later day.

Mr. David McCullough, historian and author, reminds us, *"We should never look down on those of the past and say they should have known better. What do you think they will be saying about us in the future? They're going to be saying "we" should have known better."*

These are indeed words worth remembering.

Too many historians try to tell you what you should think or how you should view an event or issue. I contend that those historians have lost their way. As you know, I dislike using the commentary of generals, politicians and citizens at the top of the food chain. It is my feeling that they are usually on a soap box promoting themselves or their position.

My faith stands fast with the common voice. Historians, authors and editors need to remain neutral and allow the past to represent itself. I continue to believe that you, the reader, are very capable of reading the letters that I have provided in this book, and my three previous books, and reaching your own opinion and conclusions on the many varied subjects. People are always a product of their time. We continue to evolve and hopefully we continue to improve. I have confidence that you will not judge the past by the present but will use these voices to gain a deeper understanding of our history during the War Between the States.

These voices are now left in your care.

Acknowledgments

I thank the ladies of the United Daughters of the Confederacy for allowing me access to the marvelous diaries, letters and journals in the archives of the Mary Walpole Brewer Library, U. D. C., Richmond, Virginia. I thank them for the permission to share these selected treasures with you. Additionally I would like to thank Teresa Roane and Betty Luck who are always present when I am doing my research and standing by to offer any assistance required.

The Special Collection Research Center of the Swem Library, The College of William and Mary, Williamsburg, Virginia, provided many of the remarkable documents that I have included in this collection. I would like to personally thank Jay Gaidmore, the Director of Special Collections, and Susan Riggs for their help and support during this project.

The Wilson Library at the University of North Carolina, Chapel Hill, North Carolina, embarked on a project to provide a scan and the transcription of a Civil War document each day during the Sesquicentennial. They created a 'Civil War Day by Day Blog' and I chose three interesting selections from almost 2,000 posted on the blog.

Thanks to Jennie Davy, my graphics wizard, for her cover design and layout work for the photography.

I would like to express my gratitude to Madeleine Eckert, William M. Harrison, Jr. and Weldon Nash, Jr. for providing pictures of their ancestors. Chuck Redding provided the Missouri bond that is the background for the cover art. The photograph of Corbin Reynolds and the other items used in the cover design are from my personal collection.

A tip of the hat to Joel Goodwin, a member of the James City Cavalry Camp #2095 of the S.C.V., who contacted several 90+ year old farm wives to determine what 'crout' might reference in an 1862 letter from the Yorktown battlefields. Thank you my friend, I am confident that your efforts found the correct answer.

Thanks to Fred Boelt, also a member of the James City Cavalry, and a historian of James City County genealogy, for his insights on Dorsey-Coupland family history.

Mrs. Billie Earnest of Norfolk, Virginia, is best known as one of the leading historians on the life of General George Pickett. Additionally she is a student of the history of the Miley Photography Studio of Lexington, Virginia. She was able to provide the key information to allow us to narrow the date of the Sarah Wood photo with her young son Robert.

As always, thank you to the folks who saved all of these marvelous documents so that our history was not lost.

Bibliography

Archives:

Brewer Library – United Daughters of the Confederacy:

    The Jesse Bates Letters

    The Nimrod Newton Nash Letters

    The John W. Robison Letters

    The J. N. & Susan Scott Letters

Special Collections Research Center, Swem Library, College of William and Mary

    The Dorsey-Coupland Papers

    The Private Thomas Head Letter

    The [Private] [S.] A. Bumgarner Letter

    The Powell Papers

The Louis R. Wilson Special Collection Library - Southern Historical Collection, University of North Carolina at Chapel Hill

    The Eli Fogleman Letters

    The Wyche & Otey Family Papers

    The General Wm. Logan Papers

Brian Green's Website: BMGCivilWar.com – scan of items for sale September, 2016.

The Julian Burnett Letter of February 16, 1862

Personal Collections:

Jeff Toalson - Selected letters of Davis, Sarah and James A. Wood

Patte Wood - "The Family History of Joseph Wood & Mary Epperson Wood of Botetourt County, " 3 July 1995, private printing.

Books:

Brigadier General James Imboden – Confederate Command in the Shenandoah, Spencer Tucker, Lexington, 2003.

Mackenzies Five Thousand Receipts in all the Useful and Domestic Arts, 4th U. S. edition, Pittsburgh, undated (1st edition in 1829).

Prey For Us All – The War Letters of Benjamin Franklin Porter, 11th Alabama: Ellen Williams – editor - Mobile, 2006.

Tennessee Civil War Veterans Questionaire, Easley, SC, 1985.

Two Soldiers – The Diary of Thomas J. Key, C.S.A., W. A. Cate – editor, Chapel Hill, 1938.

INDEX

Battles:

Bomb Manufacturing – Civilian

Cities & Counties:

Conscription, Draft, Exemptions & Substitutes:

Cost of Goods:

Food:

Lard – 55

Pie – 33

Pork – 55

Turkey – 101

Other:

Carbine – 140

Cost of a Meal – 73

Paper and Envelopes – 20

Disease & Sickness:

Cold – 101, 128

Boils – 63, 64

Breast Pain – 64

Delirious - 119

Diarrhea – 57, 59

Diphtheria – 134

Dysentery - 60

Fever – 16, 93, 101

Flux & Bloody Flux - 60

Farm Life:

Births, Sickness & Death:

Destruction of Property:

Medicine, Natural Remedies & Patent Medicines:

Laudanum – 60

Lavender Compound – 60

Lobelia Tea - 64

Muratic Acid - 24

Mustard Poultice/Blister – 23

Olive Oil – 60

Opium - 59

Rhubarb – 59

Salts to Open Bowels – 23

Smallpox Vaccination – 49

Turpentine – 65

Turpentine & Barley Water – 65

Military Units:

Braxton's Virginia Light Artillery – 35-37

Dagger Spring Company – 127

Jones' Cavalry Brigade – 67-70

Key's Arkansas Light Artillery – 83-85

Maury (Sparkman's) Tennessee Light Artillery – 19-21, 25-26, 43-45, 58-59, 147-156

Negroes:

Soldiers (U. S. C. T.) plundering and burning property – 83

Using Negroes for soldiers in the Confederate army – 135, 144

Political Comments:

"Be watchful of Yankees" - 142

"Get out of Yankeeland" (Williamsburg) – 101

Hopes of peace – 130, 136

Independence and Nationality - 144

Lincolnites – Hopkinsville, Kentucky area full of them – 19

Lincoln as only President of Northern States - 131

Morgantown [Western Virginia] is "a vile abolition hole" - 68

Need for manpower – "Tell all to come fight the Yanks" – 44

Negro is just a pretext for war – 144

Recognition by a Foreign Power – 130

States Right & Sovereign Control - 144

Treatment of Women and Children - 140

Photos:

Prison Camps:

Camp Douglas (Chicago)

Elmira (Elmira, N.Y.)

Fort Delaware (Pea Patch Island, De.)

Holding for transfer – 88

Late exchange – 71

Sick with pneumonia – 70

Fort McHenry (Baltimore, Md.)

Civilian prisoners – 87

Prison Hospital - 88

Johnson's Island (on Lake Erie in Ohio)

Parole - 88

Prisoner for 14 months – 87

Procure a parole with aid of Union General Heintzelman – 87-88

Rock Island (Rock Island, Illinois)

Deaths at the Camp – 96-97

Duty as a Nurse at Pest Hospital - 95

Eating Dogs and Rats - 96

Pest Hospital (Small Pox Ward) – 95

Rations – 95

Reduction of Rations – 95

Release to join Union Cavalry to fight Indians – 95

Shooting Prisoners by Guards (Murder) – 96-97

Point Lookout (Maryland)

Death Rate – 71

Exchange – 88

Riverboats:

Boats: (Except for the *Osceola* these are all Alabama riverboats)

Beulah – 100

Cherokee -114

Dalman – 100

Dixie – 108, 109, 110, 111, 113, 114, 115

Osceola – 61

Prarie State - 113

Reindeer – 104, 105, 106

Senator – 103, 104

Senator #2 – 107

Ailments – Carter Coupland:

Chill and Fever - 101

Cold – 101

Liver problems (brother) – 110

Rheumatism – 100

Typhoid Fever - 102

Cargo:

Corn – 112, 113

Cotton – 115

Hauling Troops – 104, 105

Passengers - 105

Cities Traveled to with the Boats:

Demopolis – 112, 113

Gainesville - 112

Mobile – 101, 102, 104, 105, 107, 114

Montgomery – 100, 106, 107, 112, 113

Selma – 100, 104, 105, 107, 112, 114

Soldiers – Camp Life:

Camp:

Clothing:

Disease in Camp:

Letters:

Letters Sent or Writing – 16, 19, 40, 49, 73, 75, 79

Write soon – 16, 20, 44, 47, 55, 74

Training:

Artillery practice - 25

Drill and Reviews – 16, 67

Picket duty – 47, 50, 78, 133

Prefer Artillery over Infantry - 43

Training as Infantry – 43

Soldiers – On the March & Battle:

Casualties and Death:

Burying the dead – 79, 80

Capturing Union Hospitals and Wounded - 76

Death Notification Letter with Map – 35-37

Death of Stonewall Jackson - 68

Flags of Truce for burial parties – 79, 80

Wounded – 91, 92, 141

Yankee dead – 75, 77, 79

Conditions on the March:

Blistered Heel - 73

Falling Out on March - 40

Feet holding up, blisters – 39

Forced Marches – 39

In Saddle 7 Days - 58

Marching – 39, 67, 74

Miles marched – 39, 68

Miscellaneous Items:

Army on the Defensive – 75, 77

Captured Cattle and Horses – 71

Captured Enemy Troops, Supplies & Armaments – 68, 71, 77

Destruction of Bridges and Railroads – 68, 71

Destruction of Oil Barges & Oil Facilities – 69, 71

Exchange of Prisoners – 135

Number of Men Remaining in our Infantry Company - 40

Set the Kanawha River Afire - 69

Writing a Letter on Horseback – 36, 38

Territorial Conditions:

Conditions in Northern Virginia – 39

Hopkinsville, Kentucky, area full of 'Lincolnites' - 19

Operating in Mountain Terrain - 69

Reactions of citizens in Maryland, 1862 – 40

Soldiers – Rations:

Beef – 55

Beef, Dried on Foot – 55, 56

Biscuit and Bacon – 39, 77

Bread – 77

Butter – 39

Coffee – 77

Cooking – 47

Corn Meal – 33

Crackers or Hardtack - 77

Ham Biscuit – 39

Sugar – 77

Without rations or short rations – 39, 58

Needs from Home:

Butter - 37

'Crout' – 33

Honey – 33

Onions – 33

Shell Beans – 33

CPSIA information can be obtained
at www.ICGtesting.com
Printed in the USA
BVHW07s0854100718
521247BV00001B/45/P